1888 Press Re
THE CURSE UPON MITRE
1888.

SPECIAL NOTICE TO THE TRADE
IN PRESS. For Immediate Publication.
THE CURSE UPON MITRE SQUARE. A. D. 1530 - 1888.
By JOHN FRANCIS BREWER.

There is a spot in the midst of one of the busiest parts of London, which is accused, whether by the power of the Evil One or by the vengeance of the Almighty we know not; but one thing we know, and that is, that deeds the foulest and crimes the vilest have been committed there on the same identical ground from the days of Henry VIII. down to our day.

Mitre Square where Catherine Eddowes was murdered, under circumstances so shameful that full particulars cannot be printed, has been cursed by villainies of even a worse kind from the year of 1530, when the High Alter of the priory Church of Holy Trinity, Aldgate, was in existence over the very spot.

What can we do to atone for those horrors that they may be stayed?

What CAN we do?

This is the cry of public lamentation and woe!

NOTICES OF THE PRESS.

"It cannot be denied that Mr. Brewer has written a clever and blood-curdling book." - Evening Post.

"A very remarkable little booklet. Is written with the best intention, and will doubtless have a fascinating interest to lovers of the tragic." -Provincial press.

"Mr. John Francis Brewer, the author of 'The Curse Upon Mitre Square, A. D. 1530-1888,' which is causing considerable interest at present, is the grandson of Rev. professor Brewer of the Rolls, Editor of the 'State papers,' etc., whom Ms. Gladstone quotes in his paper on 'Queen Elizabeth and the Church.'" -Star.

"This thrilling little tale, as condensed as a meat lozenge, is the work of Mr. John Francis Brewer, who has laid before his readers a perfect 'feast of horrors.' Having obtained possession of some very recondite and curious information concerning the precedents of Mitre Square, the author proceeds to impart his privileged knowledge in about as gruesome a tale as it has ever been our fate to read late at night, when the fire burning low and encircling one with shadows that embody the horrors one is reading, causes one to start and look up and all around in a fit of ignominious pusillanimity. ' The Curse Upon Mitre Square' boasts some literary qualities above its supreme sensationalism. 'T'is indeed a well written booklet, whose perusal we can confidently recommend to all our readers who care to have their minds agreeably thrilled by scientifically accumulated terrors." -The Gentleman.

The Curse of Mitre Square pamphlet Cover

THE CURSE UPON MITRE SQUARE

By
JOHN FRANCIS BREWER

Published by: Simpkin, Marshall and Co., 1888
(London)
John W. Lovell Co., 1889 (New York)

2015 eBook version edited and compiled
by ©Ben Hammott

ISBN-13: 978-1508564386
ISBN-10: 1508564388

Printed by Createspace

Ben Hammott is the copyright holder of this 2015 Book version.
No part of this publication may be reproduced or utilized in any form or by any means, electronic or mechanical, including photocopying, recording or by any other information storage and retrieval system, or transmitted in any form or by any means, without the written permission of the copyright holders.

Table of Contents

CHAPTER 1* — *10
 THE NEOPHYTE — 10

CHAPTER II* — *18
 THE STOLEN MEETING — 18

CHAPTER III* — *34
 PASSION EXULTANT! — 34

CHAPTER IV* — *39
 THE CELL — 39

CHAPTER V* — *44
 THE TRAGEDIES AT THE HIGH ALTAR — 44

CHAPTER VI* — *49
 ANNIHILATION OF THE MONASTERY — 49

THE CURSE UPON

MITRE SQUARE BOOK II

TWO CENTURIES AFTER

CHAPTER I* — *55
 RUMOURS OF THE APPARITION — 55

CHAPTER II* — *61
 MERRY-MAKING AT THE "MITRE" TAVERN — 61

CHAPTER III* — *69
 THE GHOST AVENGED — 69

CHAPTER IV* — *73
 IN MOORFIELDS — 73

THE CURSE UPON MITRE SQUARE

BOOK III

THE "YEAR OF GRACE," 1888

CHAPTER I — 76
WHITECHAPEL ROAD BY DAY — 76

CHAPTER II — 89
ALDGATE AT NIGHT — 89

THE HISTORY OF THE WHITECHAPEL MURDERS

AN EXTENDED ACCOUNT OF THE WHITECHAPEL MURDERS BY THE INFAMOUS JACK THE RIPPER

(18898 & 1889) *INTRODUCTION* — **101**
THE WHITECHAPEL MURDERS INTRODUCTION — 102

CHAPTER I — **106**
THE FIRST MURDER — 106

CHAPTER II — **108**
THE SECOND MURDER — 108

CHAPTER III — **114**
THE THIRD MURDER — 114

CHAPTER IV — **124**
THE FOURTH MURDER — 124

CHAPTER V	*137*
THE FIFTH MURDER	137
CHAPTER VI	*141*
THE SIXTH AND SEVENTH VICTIMS	141
CHAPTER VII	*150*
THE EIGHTH MURDER	150
THE RATCLIFFE HIGHWAY MURDERS	155
CHAPTER VIII	*174*
THE NINTH MURDER	174
CHAPTER IX	*194*
WHO IS THE MURDERER?	194

H. H. HOLMES. AMERICA'S FIRST RECOGNISED SERIAL KILLER — 213

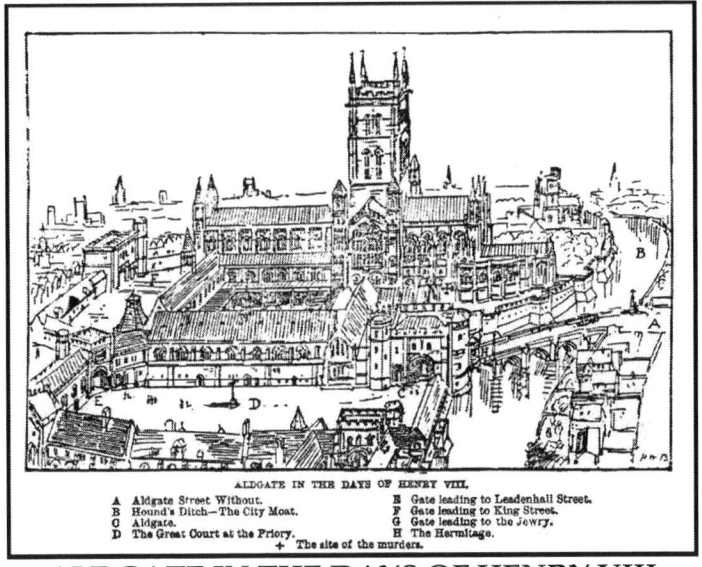

ALDGATE IN THE DAYS OF HENRY VIII.

A Aldgate Street Without.
B Hound's Ditch—The City Moat.
C Aldgate.
D The Great Court at the Priory.
E Gate leading to Leadenhall Street.
F Gate leading to King Street.
G Gate leading to the Jewry.
H The Hermitage.
+ The site of the murders.

ALDGATE IN THE DAYS OF HENRY VIII

CHAPTER 1

THE NEOPHYTE

IT was curious that, notwithstanding their power and wealth, their well acknowledged munificence, and their good fortune in other respects, the monks of Holy Trinity Church, Aldgate, were but ill at ease in the year of grace 1530. All that monks wished for they possessed. The Priory was, with the exception of Westminster, the most superb monastic institution in Middlesex. In its revenues were included the whole ward of Portsoken, four parish churches acknowledged its authority, and its privileges far exceeded those of any institution of the like kind, with the one exception named above.

It is true that its wealth had been in former times even greater, and its sway over a portion of the city more undisputed; but still so much remained, so much glory and magnificence still adhered to the monastery, that it was strange the forty monks should have cause for apprehension.

These monks were of the order of canons regular, and with greater power and greater wealth than fell to the lot of other monasteries, they, notwithstanding, escaped the open hostility of the king and his nobles. This being the case, it is plain that they were charitable and popular with their parishioners. Had any scandal attached to the Priory or its inmates, had its revenues been ill-managed, or the poor of the district adjoining cause for complaint that their wants were not attended to, then certain is it that the rapacious King Hal and his still more rapacious nobles would have marked it for destruction. Such, however, was not the case; neither king nor nobles dared lay hand on so useful and popular an institution, and Prior and monks reigned supreme, safe from the temporal power which feared to touch them.

The monks were, however, unhappy, and knew well the cause of their uneasiness. In the beginning of the year a rumour had readied the Prior that one of the forty had been seen in an adjoining church under very suspicious circumstances.

What these were the Prior did not deem fit to mention; all he attempted was to discover the delinquent who was so likely to bring discredit on his fellows. This was no easy matter, and the conduct of the forty being, as a rule, so exemplary, the Prior—easy-going, weak-minded man that he was—soon abandoned his search, and dismissed the rumour as unfounded.

Viewed from the events which afterwards occurred, it was a great misfortune to the monastery of Holy Trinity that Prior Handcock was at this juncture its chief. Not that the Prior was a bad man; his faults were not those which would disgrace an ordinary individual, but they were eminently such as incapacitated him for rule. He was very unsuspicious, very frightened of an intellect superior to his own, and very liable to favouritism. The forty monks were, taking them as a whole, a strong-minded, intellectual, and hard-headed set, and consequently he feared making his authority felt. It is, however, but fair to Handcock to mention that the men were apparently as good as they were clever, and performed cheerfully the by no means easy tasks allotted to them.

The Prior's favourite was generally the man who had last entered the monastery, and who came fresh from the pleasures, cares, and turmoils of life. There was much that was cheering in this habit of the Prior, and it often turned out well. The tranquillity, the freedom from petty worries, the probabilities of future reward, the even tenor of the monkish life, were put before the young man with no little eloquence by the kind Prior, and the youth felt satisfied, and stifled any wish to return to the world and its wicked ways. But there was also a danger in this partiality.

Handcock would never recognise that of all his flock the latest comer was the most liable to err; never could he bring himself to believe that the neophyte might not be a saint; the young man was never suspected, a cloak of protection was thrown over him, and he felt secure from punishment. Now if the neophyte was a good man, as of course was generally the case, all was well; if, however, as must sometimes happen in every institution, he was a black sheep, his misdeeds were often undiscovered and, if possible, overlooked, and thereby likely to bring great disgrace on the monastery.

In the year before this narrative commences, a young man of great promise entered the Priory of Holy Trinity. His appearance attracted attention, and when he conversed he infatuated his hearers with the eloquence and charm of his discourse.

Of spare frame, though not short, he looked delicate, but the head bespoke great power, and told of strong passion, and no unusual capacity for good or evil.

Martin, for such was his name, was very dark, with thick black hair, eyebrows that met and gave to the face a somewhat sinister look, which was partly corrected by the perfectly straightforward-looking blue eyes, which is occasionally seen in very dark persons.

The nose was aquiline, but too thin, and the mouth, the worst feature in the face, firmly closed and not unfrequently hidden by the hand. This was the more curious, as Martin possessed the whitest teeth imaginable, beautiful in their regularity and perfection.

When not conversing, Martin's appearance gave the impression of an intellect debased by cunning and evil passion. When, however, he spoke, his eloquence and

manner dispelled this, and intellect only was discernible.

Such was the neophyte and favoured *protégé* of Prior Handcock.

Great pains were taken to interest Martin in his new duties, but at first no special work was allotted to him. The monks realised that he was no ordinary man, and though, as a

rule, they did not favour new comers, they for once approved the Prior's selection of

a favourite, and regarded him as the coming light of the monastery.

It was soon evident that Martin's career would be that of a preacher, and so well did he work and so exemplary was his character, that the Prior, after consulting the other monks, decided that the more onerous duties should be waived in order that he might pursue such studies that would befit him for an orator.

Martin progressed very rapidly under the treatment of the good monks, and made himself a great master of rhetoric. His natural polish of manner and silvery voice held him in good stead, and his expressive face emphasised the thoughts that he uttered.

The Prior, however, discovered that his young *protégé* took but little interest in the works of the Fathers, and made tardy progress in theology. Everything was done to make Martin conversant with the burning questions of the day; no pains were spared to enlist his sympathy and talents in the religious cause in which all were interested, but to no avail. Martin listened to his instructors, apparently pondered over what they said, but was dull and sullen when theology, dogma, or the great cause were subjects of their counsel. The Prior perceiving the uselessness of his instruction at last gave way, and allowed his pupil to pursue his study of rhetoric according to his bent, but insisted that he should possess a fair knowledge of theology before being allowed to preach in public in the great church of Holy Trinity.

Martin's companions were, as we have stated, intellectual and good men. They performed their routine duties, both religious and temporal, in a manner which brought credit on themselves and happiness on their flock; but at the time in which this narrative is cast an unscrupulous and very able monarch hungered for the wealth of this most wealthy monastery, and it was said that he was only waiting for a fitting opportunity to stretch forth his greedy hand and grasp the prize.

The king employed dirty men to do his dirty work, and many of his tools possessed the wily cunning and insatiable thirst for gold which distinguished their master.

Foremost among these men was Thomas Audley, Speaker of the House of Commons, to whom the king was in debt and anxious to repay. Audley had an old grudge against the Priory of Holy Trinity, and had bargained with the king that should an opportunity occur and the monastery be suppressed, the proceeds should go to paying off this old debt.

The enmity of Audley was well known to the monks, who recognised in him their secret foe; but they felt no alarm so long as their reputation stood high with the people of the city.

Such was the condition of affairs when the strangest rumour reached the ears of the Prior. The monks were not told the nature of this rumour at first; all they knew was that, if true, it boded ill to them, and Prior Handcock, like all unsuspicious and weak men, stuck obstinately to his insane determination of keeping the information secret from the monks, and after awhile dismissed the rumour as unfounded.

In such fashion was laid the foundation for the ghastly tragedies and inhuman wickedness which have stamped one small portion of the site of Holy Trinity Church with the curse of Cain.

CHAPTER II

THE STOLEN MEETING

ALMOST facing the Abbey Church and spacious monastic buildings of Holy Trinity, Aldgate, but separated from them by Houndsditch—at the time of this narrative a broad stream of water—was a row of dwelling-houses, with gabled roofs and gardens at the back.

In one of these there dwelt a woman of about thirty, whose manner was so reserved, and ostracism from her neighbour so complete, that she was viewed with suspicion, and would certainly have been forced to live elsewhere but for the fact that she was reputed to be under the special protection of a high official of the Court.

This woman's life appeared to be quite purposeless, with the exception that twice a week she received messages from the hands of a page, to whom she delivered answers for her mysterious correspondent. The people in the neighbouring houses watched the woman's movements with intense interest, and argued rightly that she was the accomplice in some foul purpose; the livery of the page, however, protected her, and whatever may have been the scheme in which she was engaged, it was matured without interruption from the neighbouring inmates.

This prying curiosity, though it stopped short of open enmity, left no stone unturned to discover the reason of the mysterious woman's secrecy and the nature of her scheme. She was watched night and day, but beyond the advent and departure of the page, nothing was found out.

After awhile, however, their watching was rewarded by an event which, though it increased their curiosity, protected the woman still further from insult.

One evening in January, in the year 1530, when the snow lay thick upon the ground, it was noticed that a man, after leaving his horse in a neighbouring hostelry, approached the dwellings by a circuitous route as if to avoid notice, and after a careful searching look to see that he was unobserved, let himself into the house where the strange woman lived. Notwithstanding his precautions, every circumstance of the visit was noted by the neighbours, the stealthy appearance, the length of the interview, and the height and general appearance of the man himself. His departure was effected in the same stealthy manner, but on arriving at the hostelry a surprise was in store for him; the trapping and saddle of his horse had been removed, and no particulars of the robbery could be given by anyone.

The visit was repeated at irregular intervals, and always in the same stealthy fashion, the only difference being that the man altered his attire to that of a peasant; whereas on the first occasion he had been richly apparelled. He also came on foot—a precaution evidently considered necessary from the robbery of the saddle. Owing to the poor lighting of the road, and the fear to approach too near, none had seen the man's face sufficiently well to enable them to again recognise it; a fact which the inhabitants greatly deplored, but consoled themselves with the possession of the stolen saddle, and thought that by its means the name and position of the singular visitor would be made known to them.

After the fourth visit, which took place in broad daylight, the man and woman left the house together, and, avoiding the bridge opposite the monastery and Ald Gate, turned to the right and crossed Houndsditch by the bridge of Bishop's Gate, some little distance off.

This circumstance, though apparently not of great importance, greatly exercised the minds of the watchers, and suggested to them that whatever the secret was, the pair wished to avoid the monks.

Aldgate.

That this may not be unintelligible to readers, they must know that (see frontispiece) Aldgate was an approach to the monastery, through a courtyard of which it would be necessary to pass in order to gain access to the city. Now, the fact that the pair avoided this route and took the longer one over Bishop's Gate Bridge, was proof that they did not wish to be seen by the inmates of the monastery. After crossing Bishop's Gate Bridge the pair escaped the vigilance of the watchers.

Bearing to the left, the route taken was along Bishopsgate Street, through St. Mary Axe into Leadenhall Street, passing the stately tower of St. Mary Undershaft,(1) when finally they approached the little church of St. Catherine Cree, adjoining the Abbey buildings.

Southwest Prospect of Parish Church of St. Catherine Cree in Leadenhall Street.

The man showed a warrant and was allowed to ascend the tower of this church, which commands a good view of the cloisters and outbuildings of Holy Trinity. The singular part of the affair was that the woman was allowed to accompany him; a very rare privilege, and one which could only have been granted by reason of the importance of the warrant or the high official position of the man himself.

The monks were at recreation in the cloisters, but after awhile emerged into the open court, and the man who had impatiently awaited for this event pointed them out to his companion and bade her watch intently. In little groups the monks marched slowly to the transept door of the great church, which, when opened, emitted the solemn strains of the distant organ.

The man again grew impatient. It was evident he was watching for one who had not yet appeared. As far as was possible, from the distance he scrutinised the face of each monk, and as the last two figures emerged into the court he awoke the flagging interest of his companion, and bade her mark the younger of the two.

Martin was engaged in serious converse with the Prior. The strongly-marked features were quite visible from the tower, and the woman, after gazing at him earnestly for about a minute, satisfied her companion that she could not forget the face. On descending the tower the pair immediately separated and went in opposite directions.

After the event just recorded, the woman frequently attended the services in the great monastic church, and had the worshippers been less devout and attended less to their prayers, they might have noticed that her gaze was invariably fixed on the neophyte whenever he was present, all his movements being watched with unflagging interest.

Not only did the woman attend the church in service time, still more frequently was she there on less public occasions, especially in the mornings and evenings when the monks were reciting their offices, such as Prime, Mattins, etc. But whether the church was full or empty, her interest was centred on Martin. For him and him alone did she attend the Church of Holy Trinity.

Several months elapsed before the scheme progressed one jot. Many times did the mysterious man visit his accomplice. Long consultations they had together, but apparently nothing came of them. Evidently the intention of the woman was to get Martin by himself, probably to speak to him; but this was difficult to accomplish.

When engaged in their temporal duties the monks went their respective ways, one to one occupation and a second to another, and so on. But Martin being the youngest, and in training, had no mission entrusted to him. The monks were generally together when in church; one hour a week, however, each spent in solitary prayer before the altar, and the woman, when she discovered this, resolved to note the hour and wait till Martin's turn came, and thus obtain an interview.

She found, in addition, that these hours for solitary prayer were fixed, that is to say, each monk knew beforehand when his time would come to betake himself to the church to offer up his devotions before the high altar. Six times did the woman enter the church to be disappointed, but on the seventh she was more fortunate, and saw Martin in the sanctuary alone, but to her dismay a few people remained in the church and frustrated her design. And after waiting patiently for an hour, longing for them to depart, she saw the neophyte go back into the monastery, and thus again was she foiled in her purpose.

For a week the church was free from her evil presence, but in the following week, on the same day and the same hour, she betook herself to the place of quest, confident now of ultimate success.

It was late in the evening, nearly eight o'clock and quite dark, but the woman needed no light. She knew her way as well as the most saintly of worshippers. As she approached the church, the moon, which had been obscured, suddenly reappeared and lit up the stately magnificence of the building, and in spite of herself the woman paused and gazed upon the scene. As big as a cathedral, cruciform in shape, and of perfect symmetry, the monster church of Holy Trinity was, with the exception of the Abbey of Westminster and the Cathedral of St. Paul, the finest building of the metropolis.

Holy Trinity Church.
(In 1899, the parish of Holy Trinity, was merged into St Botolph)

Mysterious and solemn it looked on this night, and the great tower, with that almost human expression, seemed to bid her to depart and not disturb its venerable presence. The woman wavered a minute in her resolution, but stifling her scruples she entered the church and saw the young monk kneeling in the sanctuary. Again she wavered, so awe-inspiring were the surroundings; the great massive pillars supporting the rounded arches of the Norman nave, the symmetrical grace of the late Gothic clerestory, the long decorated chancel, with the solitary figure bending in prayer just visible in the gloom, Composed a picture of such impressiveness that she could but wish that another had been entrusted with the work.

She approached the sanctuary, and the rustle of her dress disturbed Martin, who looked round, displeased at the interruption; she beckoned to him, and, his curiosity awakened, the monk responded and went to the steps of the sanctuary. Perceiving, however, that the woman was not in want of help, and suddenly remembering his duty and the suspicious nature of the woman's approach, he was about to retire, when she removed the head-dress which had partly concealed her features, and Martin was instantly struck with the remarkable similarity of her face to his own.

The same black hair, the same aquiline nose and firmly sealed lips, and, still more remarkable, she had that habit of shielding the mouth before and after speech which he had so vainly tried to cure himself of when studying rhetoric. He asked her what she wanted of him, when, taking from her mantle a small scroll of parchment, she handed it to him and bade him attend her on the morrow in the church of St. Catherine Cree hard by. Having delivered her message, the woman disappeared, leaving Martin astonished and nervous at so curious an interruption to his meditation.

The monk felt it his duty to take no notice of the summons and destroy the scroll, but he was seized with overmastering curiosity to read it, and then determined to attend the woman on the morrow—a fatal resolve, pregnant with terrible consequences to himself, and still more terrible consequences to others.

On the following day the inhabitants of the gabled houses, ever on the alert whenever the doings of their mysterious neighbour were concerned, described her again leaving her home with her companion, and this time they resolved that the pair should not escape them. The saddle and trappings had given rise to great discussion, and more than one person had suggested a name for the owner, but the discussions were conducted in secret, a necessary precaution in those troubled times. The liberty of the subject was little understood in those days, the power of the king was almost unlimited, the Court was subservient and corrupt, the nobles plotted one against the other, and the party favoured by the king invariably gained the upper hand. The people wisely held aloof from politics, were time-serving to a degree, and accepted changes without murmur. Woe to the man who questioned the doings of a king's favourite. If noble, his estate was in danger; if commoner, his life! Bluff King Hal(2) ruled with an iron hand, and was not too scrupulous in his dealings.

King Henry VIII.

In fear and trembling one or two of the boldest followed the mysterious couple and tracked them to the church of St. Catherine Cree, where the woman had arranged to meet the monk. None dared to follow into the church, and were about to depart, when a muffled figure brushed past them and stealthily took the same direction as the other two. Though the people stood in awe of the man who visited their silent neighbour, judging him to be some noble or State official, they did not fear this muffled figure, so quickly going back to the entrance of the church, they traced him before he could evade them.

St. Catherine Cree Church

Notwithstanding his attempts to shield his features, they recognised the monk, whose appearance was well known to them, though they were ignorant of his name.

Now that an inmate of the monastery should be so evidently in league with the suspicious pair, much puzzled them; perhaps after all no harm was meant. Had they not better abandon their watchings?

But why had the monk shielded his features and avoided their scrutiny?

They went home and pondered over these things, and concluded to warn the Prior, and after discussing the best means of doing so, decided that the meeting of the monk in the church of St. Catherine Cree should be told, but no mention made of the strange man, as it might bring trouble upon them.

In such fashion, and not very intelligibly stated, this meeting was a day or two afterwards made known to Nicholas Handcock, and for a time caused him grave anxiety. The forty monks were assembled together and questioned. Handcock informed them that one of the number was reported to have entered the neighbouring church under circumstances such as would bring disgrace and scandal on them all.

The wrong-doer was earnestly exhorted to confess, in order that further trouble might be avoided. The monks looked grave and troubled at the news. Their feeling of security left them. Was it possible that they harboured a black sheep among them?

They could not believe it; each was so earnest and attentive to his duties.

After awhile, however, their suspicion rested on Martin, for no especial reason except that, being the youngest and least known, he was most liable to err. As usual, the Prior refused to suspect his favourite, and forbade the monks to harass Martin with their questions, and thus to the folly of one man and the curiosity of another were to be traced the ghastly tragedies which so soon occurred.

(1) 1831 description: 'St Andrew, Undershaft, is situated at the southeast corner of the street called St Mary Axe and Leaden Hall Street. There was a church on this site dedicated to the same site as early as the year 1362, which was pulled down in 1532, and the present church erected in its room, at the expense of William Fitz Williams, who was sheriff in 1507.

It derives its name of Undershaft from a very lofty Maypole, anciently called a shaft, which was annually raised in the street near to it on Mayday, and was higher than the steeple.

The church is a plain Gothic structure with a well lighted body, and the square tower, with pinnacles at the angles, and a campanile with six bells within them.

It is a rectory, in the gift of the Bishop of London, and is celebrated as containing the monument raised in memory of the faithful and able historiographer of the city, John Stowe...[1]

In 1562, St Mary Axe united with St Andrew Undershaft. It belonged to Aldgate Ward and/or Bishopsgate Ward. St Mary Axe belonged to Bishopsgate Ward.

1848 parish description: St. Andrew Undershaft with St . Mary-Axe, are parishes of the city of London Within the Walls. The patron is the Bishop; They are parishes within the poor-law union of the City of London.

(2) King Henry the Eighth, whom it has been too much the fashion to call "Bluff King Hal," and "Burly King Harry," and other fine names.

CHAPTER III

PASSION EXULTANT!

AFTER his first year's training, Martin became curious in manner. His mind wandered. His interest in study slackened. No progress was made. He was subject to shaking fits, which weakened his by no means strong frame. His face twitched, and the expression changed in a sudden, almost unnatural fashion. One minute his heavy brow was bent as if in sinister thought; the hand instinctively stole up to the mouth, and tried to hide that telltale organ. The blue eyes wandered as if frightened to fix their gaze on any object, and at such a time he looked the incarnation of evil. Another minute and this was changed. The brow, though heavy, looked that of a clever, not a base man, the blue eyes looked straight at their object, and if he spoke, the beautiful voice disarmed suspicion and adverse criticism. Had a man possessing a knowledge of physiognomy studied Martin's face and its changes of expression, he would have arrived at one of two conclusions—either that he was a clever dissembler or a man possessed of fierce passions not yet quite under his control; a man who might turn out a saint, but would stop short of no crime if evil got the upper hand, the almost convulsive changes denoting that at present neither good nor evil claimed the man, but that each was struggling for the mastery.

Prior Handcock knew nothing of physiognomy, and regarded his favourite as a man of weak health, at present overworked. The kind but injudicious man knew his pupil not one jot, and prescribed for him the worst of all things—rest.

When working hard and his powerful mind interested, Martin's nobler passions lent weight to the intellect, and gave to it a daring most like genius. When at rest and the mind relaxed, the baser passions were liable to seize the imagination and fill it with unholy thoughts, and change the genius to the fiend.

One power, however, the Prior possessed—the power of kindness. Of his inner self and the recent interview the monk did not tell the Prior; but with these exceptions, all other matters were discussed between them.

Oh, terrible pity that all was not told! Unutterable woe that now, when not too late, Handcock was not enabled to guide aright the passionate man to ward off temptation! Many a time was the neophyte minded to tell all, and almost did so after his interview with the woman in St. Catherine's. There was then not much to tell.

Mere curiosity begot the fault which Martin was too weak to confess. Formerly the Prior's kindness to his pupil might have lent him greater strength, but infinitely more was now required. A new and great temptation now assailed the man. The good resolve put off became more difficult to accomplish. The terrible passions had now begun to gain the upper hand, and were pointing out the pleasing downward course that ends in sin.

The one bright episode in this narrative of woe may now be recorded. The Prior's kindness met with some return. Martin grew to revere him much in the light in which a son regards his father, and it was at this time that the Prior questioned him on his former life before entering the monastic career.

A tale of poverty it was—of a boyhood without parents; but in his youth a change occurred. A man of high position caused him to be educated, and, unknown to him, doled out sufficient money for the purpose. Who this benefactor was he had no suspicion, but was told that when he should be old enough he was to become a monk at Holy Trinity, Aldgate.

This was all he knew concerning himself, and of his relations one only did he remember—a sister, a little older than himself, whom he had not seen for years.

The Prior and Martin took long rambles together, and, notwithstanding the disparity in years and station, entertained for one another sincere regard. But, with many and varied duties to attend to, Handcock did not see his pupil more than once or twice a week. By his orders Martin was put on the sick list, and spent the greater part of his time alone, and having been now over a year in the monastery, was allowed greater freedom, and could go much where he liked, provided he was present at the various services of the church. And so the time passed on until he again met the dark woman who had given him the scroll, in the same place—St. Catherine Cree, and this time alone. The scroll was produced, and Martin, flattening it out, read the contents and asked the woman what she had to tell him. She temporised, and the keen intelligence of the monk perceived that other designs occupied her mind—another object had prompted her to seek the interview. Had he left on discovering this, the terrible events which this narrative chronicles would never have happened; but he lingered, and looked at the woman who had dared so to deceive him.

This was the climax in Martin's life; the conflicting emotions which raged his system, the mighty passions which swayed the mind, and prompted it now to good and now to evil, put forth all their opposing strength;

virtue and vice engaged their forces in a final, fierce fight, from which one or other would emerge the victor.

Formerly the conflict had been waged in the imagination only; no great visible temptation had assailed the senses. Now came that mighty strain on the will, which the mind had foreseen and knew to be inevitable.

The woman had intended to keep up an interest in the scroll, but had failed, and faltered under the keen, penetrating gaze of the monk, and, with that subtle cleverness which often accompanies a depraved but high intelligence, realised that the time was ripe to show her hand and appeal directly to the passions of the man.

Like on the first occasion of their meeting, she threw off her head-gear and returned Martin's passionate gaze. That look was all that passed between them, but it told of guilty passion, of a secret sympathy, of the success of her scheme to the woman, and of the victory of evil in the man.

CHAPTER IV

THE CELL

HAD the prying curiosity of the people been able to penetrate into the house occupied by their silent neighbour in the evening of the event just re-corded, they would have seen her in evident grief; tears, perhaps of compunction, stole down her cheeks, and sorrow at the guilty part she was playing was no doubt felt by the woman.

Could she now in safety have abandoned her wicked course she would have done so, but the villain who hired her was not to be baulked of his purpose. Whatever her reflections were she was not long allowed to pursue them undisturbed; the door of her room was opened, and, without any further introduction, her employer entered.

Angry words passed between them; the woman wished to retire from the hateful plot, but the man was obdurate, threatened her with every punishment if she deserted the cause, and finally gained the upper hand. Being reassured of her allegiance, he ordered her, when quite certain of Martin's love, to make him leave the monastery and for her to be seen in his company at certain public places, which were specified, and finally to leave him, it being the object of the man to bring disgrace upon the monastery.

The victory of evil passion in Martin's strong character at first deadened in him every right feeling, and led him to gloat over the thought of leaving the monastery, and eloping with the woman whom he loved with a fierceness only possible in a man of such passionate temperament. He longed for the week to pass and the day to arrive when he was again to meet her. Should he achieve his purpose then, and quit the monastery and the restraint now so loathsome to him?

The conflicting emotion being silenced, outwardly Martin was calm, greatly to the delight of the Prior, who thought his pupil had recovered from an illness, and considering that the time had now come for him to resume his duties, placed him under the instruction of Father Anselm. This was the oldest monk in the monastery, and by far the ablest. With a kindness equalling that of Handcock, he possessed a keen intellect, a great knowledge of character, and a vast experience of the world. Had Martin been placed under this holy father from the first, it is probable that his difficulties and temptations would have been foreseen and danger warded off; but now it was too late; a fiend possessed his soul and held it with an iron grip.

That sense of quiet following a decision even to sin, which Martin had felt, left him under the saint-like eloquence and charity of Father Anselm. This holy man discovered the peculiar temperament of his pupil, and with a fire and genius equal to Martin's, and a tact gained from experience and knowledge of the passions of men, he poured forth arguments and exhortations of the right kind to appeal to such a temperament. The result of this to Martin was curious; his determination to sin did not leave him, but the thought of it brought untold misery. In a few days he would meet the object of his passion in the great church at the hour put down for him to make his solitary prayer. Would he fly with her and break his priestly vow?

Would he bring such scandal on the monastery?

Was that to be the return for all the kindness shown him?

Yes. Again, did he realise the greatness of the sin?

Was his faith still active?

Was he to be the one black sheep in all the fold?

Again, yes! Oh! mighty passion, like the torrent, regardless of all obstacles, ignoring all attempts to say thy headlong course; oh, fierce, all-consuming fire!

But the eloquent words of the aged priest went home, and though they did not cure Martin of his sinful desire, produced a misery so intense that he feared his mind would get unhinged. Four more days of suspense! He longed for the time to pass, yet would he fain put off the day.

One evening the monk fell ill, a burning sensation seized him, his brain seemed on fire, his mind conjured up strange and awful scenes, Hell seemed to open beneath him, and a laughing fiend to stretch out its bony arm to seize him. Was his reason giving way?

His excitement became intense, he beat his brow and clenched his teeth, then, as if suddenly struck with an idea, rushed to the church and paced the lofty nave and aisles, muttering curious, incoherent words. In his abstraction he did not notice the Prior, and started when that kind man, who had been disturbed at his devotion by Martin's strange manner, came up to him and tried to soothe him and bid him go to rest.

That evening, the Prior asked Martin to remain alone in his cell for a day or two, and arranged for a man to supply him with his wants.

Cooped up in that little cell the monk grew worse. For hours together he paced the room like a caged beast, and as each day began to wane, a look of exultation, of fiendish delight overspread his countenance. The nights brought him no rest; he did not cease his wanderings. He dared not sleep; his object was to count the hours, and time his appearance in the church. He did not eat, and the feeble frame got wasted; nor did he sleep, and the mind got no rest. The raging passion told on the wasted frame and the excited brain—the man was going mad! He knew it, but it gave him no concern. One anxiety only did he feel—to meet the woman at the hour and place appointed.

The monk had method in his madness, and knew that if seen before that fatal hour his purpose would be foiled. Those wild eyes, that excited expression, that wasted frame, spoke of insanity. Martin felt it, and longed for his time to come. Hour after hour he paced the room until the end of the day before that appointed for the meeting, when a strange thing happened. Peering out into the dark corridor to see if he was unobserved, and waiting until the deathlike stillness convinced him that no one was about, he softly closed his cell and sped down the corridors and flights of steps. The monk was absent for about an hour, and when he returned his eyes gleamed with a savage and a mad delight. What was that hidden object which gave him so much concern?

Why did he stay his wanderings to gaze at it with such a fierce interest?

CHAPTER V

THE TRAGEDIES AT THE HIGH ALTAR

AGAIN the gabled house, and the man and woman in earnest conversation. This time they managed to elude the watchers, and depart entirely unobserved. They took the same direction as before, and as they approached the monastery the clock of the great tower chimed the half hour after five, full an hour too soon, but they decided to go on and wait at their respective posts. The man had at first decided to leave before the woman's meeting with the monk, but changed his mind, and resolved to be at hearing distance, in case the woman faltered in her design. He asked her if she was quite assured she could induce the monk to leave, and her answer satisfying him, the pair arrived at the entrance of the church and peeped in. There were no worshippers; all was still, and the man looked about the church for a place from which he could watch the interview and be himself unseen. He found what he wanted in the nave, behind the monument to the first Lord Mayor of London, a long distance off from the place of meeting in the chancel, but the only spot which suited his purpose.

The hour of waiting seemed interminable; the woman paced the church with anxious steps, and the autumn day began to wane. Darker and darker the church became, great shadows were cast over the broad nave, the size of the building seemed doubled, and one part of it began to be enveloped in deep gloom. The woman turned with a shuddering glance from the dark corner, walked up the nave, ever and anon glancing behind her to see that the black shadow was not following her. She began to tremble with nervousness, and approached the chancel, which was bathed in light from the rays of the setting sun.

Stay! What was the crimson stain on yon altar step?

Horror! It seemed to move!

It must be blood!

Nearer and nearer it came!

It almost approached her!

A deep but brilliant red, at first a spot, it now increased till it seemed to flood the chancel with its sanguinary hue; then it died away again, smaller and smaller, till it lingered longest on the chancel steps.

Why did it not leave, that stain of crimson?

The sun gradually left the rich stained glass windows. Darker and darker the church became, but the woman thought she saw that crimson stain long after the black shadows had enveloped the great building.

Would the hour for meeting never come?

How long was she to remain in that dark and eerie place?

Stay! What was that?

The flickering glimmer of a little candle was approaching the choir from the monastery. It became more and more distinct; a figure entered the church, holding a taper. Could that be Martin? The face was wan and ghastly, the black hair was dishevelled, a raven lock fell over the face and made its ashen paleness more apparent. The monk held out the light at arm's length and peered into the church, and the woman was terrified at the ghastly figure. The face looked like that of a fiend, not a man; the eyes gleamed with a fierce and unnatural light, and seemed bursting from their sockets; the sleeves had fallen from the bony arm, which looked like that of a skeleton. What was that tiny bright speck just appearing under the folds of his habit?

She could not approach the ghost, and crept behind a pillar of the nave. The figure in the choir turned round and knelt down as if in attitude of prayer, and a gust of wind extinguished the taper, which the monk let drop with a thud.

The church was in total darkness, save for the little altar lamp, which but intensified the gloom. One, two, perhaps three, minutes passed, when a curious pale and silvery ray lit up a portion of the choir; the moon had risen to witness the foul and dreadful deed. The woman trembled, but felt that now she must perform her task.

Her eyes seemed to swim; she could scarcely guide aright her steps; but slowly and silently she approached the kneeling figure, and touched with her right hand the habit of the monk.

The man in the nave leant forward and watched the scene with terrible earnestness. How suddenly the monk had turned round! What was that bright object which he held aloft twice, thrice?

Good God, was murder being done?

The man rushed forward, but, alas! too late. The monk had seized the woman by the throat; a dozen times he gashed the face; the knife descended with lightning rapidity—pools of blood deluged the altar steps. With a demon's fury the monk then threw down the corpse and trod it out of very recognition. He spat upon the mutilated face, and, with his remaining strength, he ripped the body open and cast the entrails round about.

The man who had watched this scene of carnage now feared to approach, for the murderer held up his blood-stained knife in triumph, and, in his madness, called upon his patron saint and claimed a benediction for his deed. Exhausted, the monk now threw himself upon his knees, and mumbled a confused medley of prayer and imprecation. Then he got up and faced the villain whose scheme had been his ruin.

His thirst for blood now whetted, the monk would have killed the man, but the latter stepped aside and, pointing to the corpse, bade Martin look more closely at his victim. The woman's mouth was open, the moonlight streamed through the window, and Martin looked intently at the corpse. Maniac as he was, he saw that the roof of the mouth was gone. The striking resemblance of the woman to himself he remembered; an inspiration suddenly dawned upon him; he looked inquiringly at the ruffian opposite, and read in his countenance a confirmation of the awful thought.

An agonising cry escaped his lips, he seized the knife, and plunged it deep into his heart, and fell a corpse upon his murdered sister.

CHAPTER VI

ANNIHILATION OF THE MONASTERY

THE good monks of Holy Trinity, Aldgate, were regular in all their duties, and punctually at nine o'clock they betook themselves in solemn conclave to the church, to offer prayers that God might watch over the great city and protect it from disaster.

They carried lighted candles and, preceded by the Prior, arranged themselves in order for procession, and marched towards the transept door of their splendid abbey church, chanting the ancient Latin hymn, *Ye guardian spirits, protect the holy men from the awful sight, the murder, the suicide, the desecrated church, the scene of deeds which had perverted the hallowed building to a place accursed by God and man!*

Je-su dulcis me-mo-ri-a.

The monks shut up their church and kept the fearful deeds secret, but no happiness or rest did they know after that fatal night. Ghosts of the murdered dead haunted them; they longed to leave the accursed spot, and atone for the sin of their wicked brother.

And the man whose schemes had worked the misery, Sir Thomas Audley, afterwards to be Lord High Chancellor, what was his next step?

Threats were sent to the Prior, threats of instant exposure, if he did not surrender the monastery to the king. The poor weak Prior, beside himself with grief and misery, consulted the monks, and they counselled him to hold out, and for some time there was a sort of interregnum. All traces of the murders were apparently obliterated; and the monks attempted to burn out the stain of blood, but finding this impossible, they hollowed out the stone. This done, they sent an emissary to the Pope, and in resignation awaited for the interdict. But whether their messenger was intercepted or whether the interdict was sent is not known; certainly it was never placed upon the buildings.

Sir Thomas Audley informed the king of the murders which had taken place, which he pretended to have unexpectedly discovered, and the king, glad of an opportunity of repaying Sir Thomas for the salary owed to him as Speaker of the House of Commons, gave the Royal permission for the suppression, provided Audley could by threats induce the Prior to make a show of giving up his charge.

Audley called in Thomas Cromwell, and the two sent another message to the Prior, containing renewed threats that if the monastery were not delivered to the king, all the ghastly particulars of the murder and suicide would be made known to the peoples of the city. The Prior and monks now found it impossible to hold out longer, and gave up the splendid time-honoured church and monastic buildings to the king, under a trifling pretext which Audley had invented and forced upon them.

It is but fair to Henry VIII. and Cromwell to mention that they were ignorant of Audley's infamous plot, and had no notion that it was owing to his action that the crimes had taken place.

The monastery was suppressed, the monks turned out, and somewhat later Audley was placed in possession of the building. The poor Prior's troubles were even now not yet over. A letter of his is extant in which he complains that no portion of the seven hundred pounds a year promised to him after the suppression had been received; but how he provided for himself and the monks is not known.

Audley attempted to sell the buildings, but was not able to do so, and at last he ruthlessly destroyed the magnificent architectural pile; and, with the exception of a few arches, left no trace of the church and monastic institution of Holy Trinity, Aldgate

Ruins of Holy Trinity, Aldgate.

Both during the process of destruction and many years after that event, no one, unless obliged, would approach the spot where the high altar and chancel of the church had once existed. It was rumoured that every night, between the hour of twelve and one, a dark young man appeared in the garb of a monk and always pointed to a spot, and uttered strange prophecies of terrible events that must occur there. The people got wind of the story of Martin and his sister, and for many generations the spot was considered cursed.

Woe to anyone who would live on that spot; woe to him, who remained there at night and out of reach of help!

END OF BOOK I

THE CURSE UPON MITRE SQUARE

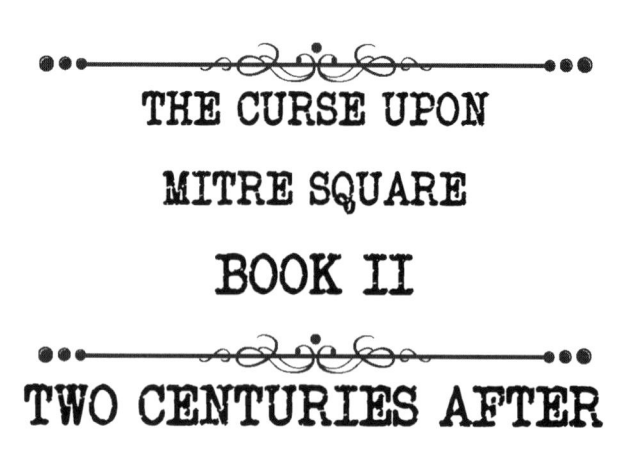

BOOK II

TWO CENTURIES AFTER

CHAPTER I

RUMOURS OF THE APPARITION

"**HOW** comes it, man, that thy friend Jack Walton is never with thee now?

The tavern misses him; his cheery face was always welcome; and when I think of it, thou art thyself flat sorry company, nowadays."

The jolly, red-faced host of the '*Mitre*' liked not a dull and quiet guest; good food and drink, he used to say, were wasted when they loosened not the tongue in anecdote or song.

"Jack has gone, and I'll soon follow him," was the dismal answer.

"Ye mean to tell me that Jack the fearless, the mighty toper, the jolly drunken rogue, has turned craven and thrown up his employ?"

"Landlord, ye have hit it; the others are going too, and if ye take my advice ye'll shift the '*Mitre*' to another place."

"Fool, take thy womanish fears to others; the '*Mitre*' and Will Railton will not shift for Papist ghost or other foolery; but hark thee, Grale, a week to-morrow I shall prepare a feast, to which ten or twelve young bloods from town will come.

You, Grale, and your fellow-workers at the stable, have been my friends; help me now prepare this feast, and lend me your daughters as waiting-maids; my own lass, Rose, who will be here of course, will look after the others, and see that no harm comes to them."

Grale promised to send his daughter to help prepare the feast, and asked his host in what manner he meant to amuse his wild young guests.

"Ay, that is what I wished to tell you. Ye know yon spot, beneath the arch, where the Papist monk killed his sister and himself. I shall take them there, and you, Grale, or some other such fool who believes the story, must recount it to them; by which time I shall have primed them well with wine. When it is quite dark, they shall all move out, terrible noises shall be made, and as all are waiting for the ghost, my daughter Rose shall spring into their midst, which, if I mistake not, will make them merry and contented with their visit.

Grale looked serious, and thought no good would come from tampering with the ghost, but knew of old that Railton of the '*Mitre*' regarded the story of the monk as a myth, and laughed at those who differed from him. Grale paid for his little meal, and went out into the courtyard in front of the tavern and rejoined his companions.

These men worked in the stables which were built up with the few rounded arches and Norman columns, relics of the once glorious church of Holy Trinity.

The spot reported to be haunted was just outside the stable, furthest from the court, exactly where the altar steps of the church had formerly existed. The ghost was said to appear on this spot between twelve and one at night on certain days, and mutter strange warnings, and in other ways disport himself as is the wont of ghosts.

All the people in the district firmly believed the story, except the jolly host of the '*Mitre*'; but there were diverse opinions as to the day or days of the appearance, some contending that they had seen it on Sunday nights, others—the majority—on Mondays.

Now though Railton was the only sceptic, and thus formed a party by himself, the other people of Aldgate Ward formed themselves into two factions—those who believed in the Monday appearance—the men engaged in the stables and a few others—and those who swore that Sunday was the ghost's night.

A wag from town, when told of the affair, had declared that the majority were Sunday believers, because, being virulent anti-Papists, they wished to think the monk had broken the Sabbath law, the wag adding that this fact exercised the people's minds more than the murder, which they held to be an ordinary occurrence with the priests of old.

However this may be, party feeling ran high, and Railton was wont to declare the Monday folk would sooner believe in no ghost at all than that it should appear on Sunday, and *vice versa*. But he was wrong; there were solid foundations for a belief, though many might mistake the day, and in after years the host himself believed the story, and held that the fatal spot was indeed accursed by God and man.

"Jack gone! Then I suppose he has seen the monk," a brother worker said to Grale.

The latter nodded, and added, "Jack lost his wife a week after he saw the cursed Papist."

"But I've seen 'im, and nothing's come to me," remarked several of the stablemen, and Grale, who was the oldest and most learned in the ghost's ways, turned and said—"You may 'a seed 'im, so 'ave I; but that is not the point. *The man who, with a wicked purpose or to jeer at the monk, stands upon that spot between the hours of twelve and one and sees the ghost, will surely come to harm.*" The old fellow was impressive; the terms of the curse were not stated in his own words, but were a formula well known to many of the inhabitants of the Ward of Aldgate.

Certainly it was no joking matter, given the conditions which Grale mentioned. A curse did alight on the unlucky person who approached the spot with a criminal or jeering intention. The curse did not necessarily end in death, another misfortune might happen to the offender; but many and foul were the crimes which this very spot had witnessed from the year 1530 to the date in which this second narrative is cast.

Mitre Tavern

CHAPTER II

MERRY-MAKING AT THE "MITRE" TAVERN

GREAT preparations were made at the old Mitre Tavern for the advent of Railton's young gallants. Food and wine, the best that could be procured, were in readiness. The buxom daughters of the stable-men donned their prettiest gowns, and looked their brightest for the occasion. Will Railton, Grale, and others were in attendance, all primed to their duties, and anxious that the meeting should pass off merrily.

The guests were slow in arriving—not one came in time. Railton remembered with a pang that the choicest dishes would be spoilt; a punctual man himself, he had timed the cooking to be ready to the minute, and here it was full half an hour behind the hour arranged.

What with the scowlings of the cook, the kitchen-maids, and the fair waitresses, he did not know, so he said, which was in the worse state—the burnt-up capons or his own head.

But at last they came, and all together; a dissipated crew, richly dressed; men born in a good position, nobles, soldiers, and the like, polished in manners (when sober), irregular in their habits, they honoured the '*Mitre*' with their presence just once a year, in return for services Railton rendered them in their own part of the town. It may seem strange that they should travel to what was, even in those days, an unfashionable district; but Railton was a man of weight, a famous cook, a maker of good punch; a man the gallants liked to please, and secure for their own costly entertainments. Besides which, Railton was a man of wit, and always prepared some amusement for his guests. Their jaded palates liked his rich cheer, their worn-out sense of fun was tickled with his sparkling wit; they enjoyed their day, and came again when asked.

These were days of hard drinking; not in the sense in which this degenerate nineteenth century understands the term. Drinking was then an art, confined principally to the rich. Drink did not claim its thousand gutter-victims, as at present.

The poor got drunk, of course, but not to the same extent as now.

The gentlemen of those days were careful as to the quality of the wine they drank, but not the quantity; they vowed a man ill-bred who did not take his share. But just as they would not cross swords with a man of blood inferior to their own, and regarded duelling as a pastime only of the *"gentle,"* so also did they consider drunkenness a privilege peculiar to themselves.

They sent their servants to the lock-up for a tipsy peccadillo, they drew long pious faces at the luxury of monks, and fell beneath their tables every day, which became them as true gentlemen.

A merry, worthless set that was which Railton brought together: Lord Wareham, member of the Mohawk gang; Sir Jocelyn Cholmondeley; Jack Mounteagle, Percy Poins, and others, all in the fastest, loudest set. They ate their fill, drank deep, and joked the pretty waiting lasses.

Hilarity was the order of the day. The jokes went round with every dish, and the serving-maids, though teased to death, declared it bright and merry fun!

When to eat more was impossible, Railton rose and bade them fill their glasses, while he proposed a toast with a song:

Here's a health unto His Majesty;
With a fal lal la!
Damnation to his enemies;
With a fal lal la!
And he who would not pledge this health,
I wish him neither wit nor wealth,
Nor yet a rope to hang himself;
With a fal lal la!

Jacobites they were, one and all. And how lustily all joined in the rowdy *fal lal la*, and how the elements of seriousness and fun intermingled in the then popular ditty When quiet was resumed, the host again rose, and with a merry twinkle in his eye, drew himself up, and in a mocking-serious tone exclaimed—"Gentlemen, have ye heard of our ghost in yonder part of town? I see ye have. Let's drink to him. Monk Martin, Papist priest, here's to your health; mind come and visit us to-night."

Grale and the other stablemen stood aghast at such temerity, and Railton, seeing their fears, proclaimed them with derision to the company. A shout of laughter greeted this. The gallants had drunk deeply, and were getting quite uproarious.

Lord Wareham now got upon his legs—"Will Railton, you have proposed a toast; let me propose another: ' Drink, gallants all, to buxom Mistress Rose, and death to him who says she's not the prettiest maid in Aldgate.'"

This was followed by great applause, and Railton, who studied well the pleasures of his guests, proposed a dance, and removed the tables and chairs for that purpose.

The young men who, a few minutes ago, appeared half tipsy, threw off their rowdy gaiety, and went through the various evolutions of the dance with the utmost ease and grace. The untaught damsels looked at their elegant partners with evident admiration, and tried to imitate their courtly manners.

Mistress Rose being the prettiest maiden present, and the daughter of the host, of course came in for the greater attention, and these jaded men, who had ceased to care for dancing with the well-taught damsels of their own class, eagerly sought Railton's daughter for a partner, and rivalled one another in their gallant speeches to her.

"Host Railton, dost thou think the Papist Martin will obey thy summons?"

"Thou'dst better ask the stablemen, my friend. Here, Grale, will the ghost appear to-day on yonder spot?"

"Many ha' seen Monk Martin, but we canna tell for certain when he comes. But *the man who, with a wicked purpose, or to jeer at the monk, stands upon the spot, between the hours of twelve and one and sees the ghost, will surely come to harm.*"

"Tut, tut, man, stop that silly jargon. Tell us, if thou canst, whether Martin will appear or not?"

Grale feared the vengeance of the ghost, and knew what ill had come to those who jeered and disbelieved its appearance.

"Noble gallants, listen not to Master Railton's gibes! Do not, I pray thee, visit yonder spot."

The guests laughed loud and long at the old man's fears, and began to pester him with ridicule.

"Look, Grale, there is the monk behind thee. Methinks that Master Grale had better don the cowl. Turn Papist, man, and please the ghost, and save thyself from danger."

"Art thou a Sunday or Monday believer, Grale? Prophesy; tell on which of us will come the curse?"

The old man was grave and silent; he did not mind the ridicule, and feared a reckoning would come to such misplaced and sacrilegious mirth.

"Thou dost not answer, man. Did Martin break the Sabbath law?"

"I must tell the parson of thee, Grale. Thou won't accuse a ghost of crime. Fie, thou call'st thyself a Protestant."

On another occasion pretty Mistress Rose would have thought such conversation dangerous, but surrounded with such gay and noble gallants, she felt secure and happy.

By-and-by they adjourned to another room, where Railton had prepared a bowl of steaming punch.

The waiting-maids now sat down to table with the others, and more toasts and pretty speeches followed.

Rose sat between Lord Wareham and Poins, and looked from one to the other with divided admiration,

"They ought to send thee, Mistress Rose, to seek the ghost. Mine host, Will Railton, what say you? Shall thy daughter go and find the monk?"

Poins followed his lordship in his little jest. "If Martin sees thy buxom face and cherry lips and answers not thy call, then, odsbodikins, if he's Papist priest or no, a ghost he is, and I'll believe the story."

Railton answered: "Methinks if the myth which goes the round be true, the monk will have no more to do with womankind; but still, as it seems to please your wit, the damsel shall betake her to the spot, and try to exorcise the spirit."

The hour was now getting late, and Rose, much to her regret, left with the stableman to find the accursed spot. Once away from the scene of revelry, her heart misgave her. What was she doing? Going to stand on that awful site to jeer at the avenging spirit? No, she could not do it; look at the fate which had befallen so many fearless sceptics!

She spoke with Grale, and the two determined to hide in an outhouse, and see what happened. They had left the tavern very late, and the night, though dark, was then quite fine.

It was late in autumn, but not cold, and as the hour of midnight came a close feeling was noticeable in the air; the sky became dark; a storm had been presaged for this very night. A disturbing, fierce wind now suddenly sprang up; it shook the very stables; the moaning, soughing noise increased; a mighty gust of wind swept past the ancient Norman arches, and seemed to make them totter.

"Oh, leave me, Grale, and go and warn yon gallants of the night!"

"No, Mistress Rose; I stir not from this place. The monk is coming. Look not on the fatal spot! Oh, save us from the sight! I did not jeer thee, priest. Send not the curse upon my aged head."

"Then I will go to father, and tell him not to come."

"Thou shalt not do so, damsel. Hark! Listen to the storm! A deed of vengeance is at hand. Look, maiden, at the fierce and sudden flames! The heavens are on fire!"

The old man held the girl in a tight grip, and would not let her move. She tried to force herself away, but was not able, and Grale at last persuaded her that Railton and his guests were not likely to leave the tavern in such a fearful storm.

CHAPTER III

THE GHOST AVENGED

AFTER the departure of the maids, the men drained the bowl of punch, and Railton brewed them another. They soon began to show evidence that the second howl was too much for them; one dropped beneath the table, another fell asleep, but Lord Wareham and Poins emptied the bowl, and were still comparatively sober.

Railton went to the window and looked out.

"It's raining, my lord, and I see a storm's approaching. Had we not better wait a little, until the weather clears?"

"No, no, unless the ghost does not appear in storms. What weather does he generally bring?"

"Well, my lord, they say the monk appears in a flash of lightning, and if that be true he might be appearing in a dozen places now."

Poins woke up the others, not in a very gentle manner, and said—"A little cold water will do us all no harm, and if you are ready, Railton, lead the way while I help these gallants to move."

The men were all put upon their legs. Lord Wareham, Poins, and Railton helped them along; and when they got outside the pouring rain soon sobered them.

Two centuries had indeed altered this part of Aldgate ward. The monastic buildings and church of Holy Trinity had all gone, except for a few rounded arches and huge Norman pillars which, as before mentioned, had been partly roofed over as stables. Near these was the old "*Mitre*" tavern, which looked on to a court; and close by was an ugly red brick church, St. James', surrounded with a small churchyard. The scene of Monk Martin's crimes was just outside the stables—a large slab of stone, and near to a remnant of a decorated arch and wall of the old chancel.

The men shivered from the wet, and Poins exclaimed, "The monk must have gone to the brimstone pit to seek the earth on such a rainy night."

But both gallants and host soon ceased their prattling; it was evident that the worst of the storm had yet to come. The thunder grew louder and louder, the rain came down in torrents, and forked flames were shooting from the heavens, and lit up the ruins of the once stately church.

Nearer and nearer came the storm, when a terrific peal of thunder made the bravest of them quail. Now was the storm right above them, and raging with ungovernable fury. The wind howled like a fierce beast in pain, the heavens seemed to open and cast down streams of liquid fire. Listen to that fearful crash! A mighty battle was being waged above; or was an angry God hurling His anathemas at the sins and crimes of men? Could the elements increase their fury? The liquid flames seemed to unite and concentrate their force; they struck that fatal slab of stone, once, twice; it seemed to disappear, and then a hellish cry—the pitch-black cloud seemed resting on that awful spot!

The men were almost dead with fear.

What was yon cloud?

Why did it not move?

The tempest seemed to gather round it, the lightning struck at it a dozen times.

It slowly lifts and utters a hollow, dreadful laugh. Is it ghost or fiend?

It seems diminishing in size. Horror! It assumes the shape of a man! What is it that it holds aloft?

Again the lightning struck at it, and its ghastly head was seen.

Another crash of thunder, and a naked arm appears, holding a blood-stained dagger.

Oh, what is it that it strikes with such a demon fury?

Why that final, dreadful cry?

The spectre seemed approaching them; they shriek with terror, but cannot escape. Railton seizes two of them, and drags them from the spot. Why could he not take the others?

A dark and mighty mass is moving; it splits into a thousand bits, it flies at them with fierce spite, it strikes and kills, and buries its disfigured slain!

CHAPTER IV

IN MOORFIELDS

"**I TOLD** ye all about Monk Martin's ghost."

"Yes, Grale. We know about the wicked monk."

"Well, master, what think ye happened on the cursed spot not twenty hours ago?"

"Tell us, Grale; ye know we all believe the ghost."

The old man, with a look of triumph in his weather-beaten face, now got up and said——"Ye know about the curse. *The man who, with a wicked purpose, or to jeer at the*

monk, stands upon that spot——"

"Tut, Grale we know about the curse."

"Well masters, ye know Will Railton of the '*Mitre*' tavern, Aldgate. He asked a dozen gallants from yonder part of town. They came and made merry, and jeered at Martin's ghost. I warned them not to do it, but ye know the sort of men. Well, in the middle of the storm Will Railton took them to the cursed spot. Ye also know that *the man who, with a wicked——*"

"Hurry on, friend Grale, we know all that."

"Well, when the storm was at its worst they saw the ghost. They say he struck that ancient arch. It fell upon the gallants, and killed and buried ten of them."

This conversation took place in Moorfields, some distance from the tavern. Grale had left Aldgate and sought employ elsewhere. Will Railton, Lord Wareham, and Poins, the men who had escaped from the falling ruin, probably because they were the most sober, now believed in Monk Martin's ghost.

No more gallants were seen in the '*Mitre*' tavern. Railton left, and took another inn, and vowed the spot indeed accursed!

END OF BOOK II

THE CURSE UPON MITRE SQUARE

BOOK III

THE "YEAR OF GRACE," 1888

CHAPTER I

WHITECHAPEL ROAD BY DAY

IF a foreigner were now to visit this great metropolis with the object of studying it as a vast social problem, he would find it, broadly speaking, divided into three parts—the abode of wealth, the world's mart, and the abode of poverty.

Further, he would discover that the abode of wealth knows nothing of the abode of poverty, scarcely recognises its existence, and even tries to take from it the common name of London; that the West would if it could ignore the East, and succeeds in suppressing all knowledge of the appearance, conditions of life, and difficulties of its unfortunate brother.

If he hunted up old books, and was interested in archaeology, he would see that this used not to be. That wealth and poverty once built together, that the poor man could approach the rich, and that benefit resulted to the former from the contact.

That the rich, if unselfish, gave money to the poor to improve their dwellings, and if selfish tried to remove the eyesores, filth and crime, which existed so near to their own doors.

He would discover that gradually, but more particularly lately, the rich divorced themselves from their poorer brethren, whose needs became neglected because unseen; that the two went their separate ways, and drifted farther and farther apart, until at present they had almost forgotten one another's existence.

Then, probably, he would seek the rich, and discover to his surprise that they were not uncharitable, and were the most enterprising people in the world. He would remember to have seen them everywhere in all the poor streets and back slums of foreign cities. He would be told of their mighty grants to the poor of other countries, and their untold exertions to better the condition of the savage. He would hear them describe such and such a foreign city as poor and miserable, though they would not mention the far greater poverty and squalor of the East of London.

If he went into society, he would be led to believe that the City bounded London in the East, that no one had ever been further in that direction than the Tower, that the vast outlying districts were never mentioned; and if he stated that he had travelled in the unknown region, he would be frowned at as though guilty of a social fault. Did he force the subject of the East upon the denizens of the West, and remind them of their starving

London brother, they would refuse to recognise the latter, and speak of him as if he were a bastard.

Then probably he would go and seek the people of the East, and try to find what they had done to deserve such wholesale neglect. He would find a people of good natural character, but hampered by their wretched dwellings, who found it hard to escape from their hideous surroundings; who had waited long for the help that never was forthcoming, and paid too highly for the little which they got; who did not know what pleasure meant, and had sunk into a deep despair.

Tenements - Houses for the Poor

The ward of Aldgate has perhaps seen more changes than any other portion of the old metropolitan area. The site of the glorious church and monastic buildings of Holy Trinity, it was, in the time of the first narrative, distinguished for its architectural interest. Few, on gazing at the monastery in the earlier part of the sixteenth century, could have thought it possible that so important and splendid a pile of buildings would in so short a time have almost wholly disappeared. Had it not been for the foul crimes which took place on the most sacred spot in the church of Holy Trinity, probably some part of that building would now exist and be used for the purposes of worship, as is the case with St. Bartholomew the Great, Smithfield, a church contemporaneous with Holy Trinity, though only about a fourth its size. But this was not to be; Monk Martin stamped the once hallowed edifice with the curse of Cain, and a revenging power decreed that it should be destroyed, and its site become the scene of other fearful crimes.

Good men there always are, however, who carry on an unceasing struggle against evil, and in the reign of James I. an old Lord Mayor of London, remembered with sorrow the destruction of Holy Trinity, and erected on a portion of its site the little church of St. James, Duke's Place. St. James's was indeed a poor affair in comparison with the former stately building, but we praise the spirit of the mayor who erected it, *"as a Phoenix rising out of*

the old church," and as the quaint old epitaph has it—
"He never ceased in industrie and care, From Ruins to redeem the house of Praier."

St. James's Church

St. James's was destroyed in the eighteenth century; it was, however, rebuilt, but finally disappeared about twenty years ago.

The following sketch was made when the rebuilt church had been destroyed. A small portion of the tower was still standing, surrounded by gravestones torn up and flung about in wild disorder. The church door was lying flat upon the ground, and bits of the pews were seen mixed up with fragments of window glass and brickbats. St. James's Church stood over a part of the site of the nave of Holy Trinity.

Sketch of St. James's Church Ruins
"What are they among so many?"

It is interesting to note that the whole neighbourhood of the Tower to Aldgate once presented a succession of religious houses established by our kings and queens.

There was the great Hospital of St. Katherine, founded by Matilda, Queen of Stephen, and rebuilt by the good Philippa; Eastminster Abbey, founded by Edward III.; the Abbey of the Minnies, or Minories, founded by Richard, King of the Romans; the Friary of the Holy Cross, Crutched Friars; Millman's Almshouses; the Hermitage, in Aldgate; the Papey for Aged Priests, close to Holy Trinity Priory; and others. Where are all these now?

A dock covers the site of one—St. Katharine's.

A writer in the *Gentleman's Magazine* in 1829, when this change was effected, pointed out that *"The worship of God was sacrificed to that of Mammon."* A huge railway runs over the site of another. A third is covered by giant warehouses, and the rest are built over with squalid tenements, where the poor are huddled together like beasts in a pen.

There are a few—though very few—small institutions where religion is taught, and from which charity is spread, but The Whitechapel Road, in the *"year of grace"*1888, is a sort of portal to the filth and squalor of the East. Here begins that dreary region from which healthful and legitimate pleasures seem banished, and hard and ill-paid toil to be the lifelong fate of the inhabitants. Stand in the one broad thoroughfare, Whitechapel Road, and watch the constant stream of passers-by, and try and find a happy-looking face! How dismal they all look; what a weight of care they seem to carry!

Whitechapel circa 1888

In Victorian times, most of Whitechapel and neighbouring Spitalfields was a grim warren of streets, courts and alleyways. Here some 80,000 souls eked out a miserable existence in appalling poverty and squalor. Over half the children born here died before the age of five.

Whitechapel Slum

Dark And Foreboding Alley

Early in the morning thousands pass along, to earn their daily bread. Half-starved clerks, with shiny coats, shabby hats, and pinched-in faces, presenting an appearance of beggarly gentility, that most pathetic sight of modern civilisation. Could we look into the tail-pockets of many of their black coats we should see, carefully ensconced with all privacy and care, a slice of bread which, with the addition of an apple, and eaten in some sly corner of the streets, frequently constitutes the dinner of these respected and worthy souls. And such as these, with successful tradesmen, form the *aristocracy* of a population as large as many a stately city!

Osborn-street, Corner of Whitechapel Road

Then, lower in the scale, we see the skilled mechanics, the most useful men of all; but these look gloomy now the foreigners are stepping in and making rotten goods, getting employment by working longer hours for shorter pay.

And then the factory hands, the lowest class, limping to the badly-ventilated rooms to work, perhaps for fifteen hours for a wretched little pittance. Look at their wan faces, and thin, ill-fed bodies; what a tale could they tell of misery and over-work!

And the vast army of the unemployed who loaf about the streets, stand outside public-houses, and level curses and obscene language at innocent passers-by!

Lastly, the girls. "What are they like? Are they the types of purity and sweetness that poets love to talk of?—made by the Creator to guide the rougher natures of men unto the realm of light and love? Is this group of factory girls dressed up in ribbons and feathers of garish, screaming colours, shouting foul words, and laughing loud at every man they pass, likely to refine a home?

Whitechapel Street Scene

Is this other group of shabbily-dressed girls, with care and labour stamped upon their injured faces, likely to do more than provide bare crusts for the little ones at home?

Yes, the Whitechapel Road is not a tempting place for a refined Londoner or foreigner, for it is a place where innocence no longer dwells; where the young in years are old in knowledge, though, alas! not of good, but of evil.

CHAPTER II

ALDGATE AT NIGHT

A SATURDAY evening in the East-end of London! Who that has seen this sight can ever forget it? Crowds upon crowds of dissolute men and women jog and jostle each other upon the pavements, and the roads are nearly impassable from the costers' carts, containing every conceivable article of diet, apparel, and mechanical contrivance. The men shout out the rare value of their goods in exultant tones, as if to defy comparison with their rivals further on.

How depressing is the scene! But what is that singing we hear? Two big young girls with dishevelled hair, arm in arm, brush past us—excited by drink, screaming from lungs of iron the song last heard at the '*Cambridge*' hard by.

As we walk on we pass a church with two huge lamps, vying with the public-house lights in importance and attractiveness—and these reveal a picture by one of our greatest allegorical painters. See that dear young child awe-inspired, wonderingly staring at the mosaic which he cannot understand, but vaguely feels is telling of a life widely different from that of his own debased surroundings.

But as the commemoration of the Resurrection dawns upon us, the streets suddenly become dark, for the bright lights are extinguished and the duped ones are ejected from the glittering palaces, some to stumble and totter through innumerable alleys to what is called home, and others to lounge about with apparently no object in life. Life itself seems dead in them as they live. Half-starved many of them, and homeless; without wishing it or wanting it, falling into sin—apparently unintentionally. How can we blame them? Should *we* be better?

But let us hurry out of this pandemonium into purer air. We breathe once more as we approach Aldgate's comparative quiet, and proceed westward. But why that whistle and hurrying of men to Mitre Square? Let us join them, and find out for ourselves.

There with the aid of the policeman's bulls-eye we see a sight so horrible that full particulars cannot be printed, but it is a counterpart of that which the monks of Holy Trinity saw when they arrived at that identical spot in the year 1530.

Body Discovered in Mitre Square

Measure this spot as carefully as you will, and you will find that the piece of ground on which Catherine Eddowes lies is the exact point where the steps of the high altar of Holy Trinity existed, and where the catastrophe to the ten foolish gallants occurred two centuries later.

Oh, what can we do that these horrors may be stayed?

What CAN we do?

This is now the cry of public lamentation and woe!

Is the ghost of Monk Martin still hovering over the scene of his crime?

Is the power of the Evil One still active?

Or is it the vengeance of the Almighty that has cursed this spot with a curse so awful in its results that no age can with certainty evade punishment?

Who is there so bold as to say that the one bit of ground that has sustained the weight of countless lifeless bodies, during more than three centuries, is not accursed—that there is no *Curse upon Mitre Square?*

As the pen drops from the hand cramped with writing this fearful historical narrative of crime and retribution—the brain in very sympathy and overwrought with recounting the ghastly tragedies of present and bygone times, seeks ease and rest in slumber, and in sleep the veil of the future is unfolded.

What is that white-robed procession bearing tapers and singing the Miserere? O blessed sight, behold a stream of Magdalens, with, flowing hair and downcast eyes, winding their way, as did the forty monks of old, to the accursed spot.

And as they approach it, carrying their precious ointment, behold a radiant light is in the air, reflecting a benediction on the spot below; and I see aloft the choir of Holy Trinity as it was before the curse fell upon it, restored by the Divine Architect to its old beauty and splendour, the rounded arches and the carved stalls on either side the altar. Instead of monks, I see, through the wreath of incense, a choir of angels waving their palm branches to the rhythm of the heavenly antiphon—so full of favoured promise to all wanderers in this troublesome world:—

*"THOUGH YOUR SINS BE AS SCARLET,
THEY SHALL BE AS WHITE AS SNOW!"*

*"THOUGH THEY BE RED LIKE CRIMSON,
THEY SHALL BE AS WOOL!"*

END OF THE MITRE SQUARE BOOK

(1888 Original Title)
THE

HISTORY

OF THE

WHITECHAPEL MURDERS

A FULL AND AUTHENTIC NARRATIVE
OF THE ABOVE MURDERS, WITH SKETCHES.

1888
RICHARD K FOX PUBLISHER AND PRINTER,
FRANKLIN SQUARE,
NEW YORK.

2015 eBook Version Compiled and Edited by ©Ben Hammott

1889 Reprint Included in
CHRONICLES
OF
CRIME AND CRIMINALS

Remarkable Criminal Trials—Mysterious Murders—Wholesale Murders-

Male and Female Poisoners—Forgery and Counterfeiting—Bank and Post Office Robberies—Swindlers—Highway Robbery and Railway Crimes—Daring Outlaws—Road Agents, Bushrangers and Brigands, Etc., Etc.

No. 1.

(1889 Title)
AN EXTENDED ACCOUNT OF THE

WHITECHAPEL MURDERS

BY THE

INFAMOUS

JACK THE RIPPER

BEAVER PUBLISHING COMPANY, TORONTO 1889

2015 eBook Version Compiled and Edited by ©Ben Hammott

'PICKING UP' IN THE EAST END, WHITECHAPEL.
(Original 1888 Book Image)

ILLUSTRATIONS

'PICKING UP' IN THE EAST END, WHITECHAPEL. (Original 1888 Book Image)

WAS A MADMAN PROWLING THE STREETS OF WHITECHAPEL?

HOW THEY LIVED IN WHITECHAPEL (Original 1888 Book image)

HOW THEY LIVED IN WHITECHAPEL (Original 1888 Book Image)

MARTHA TURNER (OR MARTHA TABRAM)

A WHITECHAPLE TYPE (Original 1888 Book Image)

DISCOVERY OF BODY IN BUCKS ROW.

DISCOVERY OF A VICTIM. (Original 1888 Book Image)

ALL WHITECHAPEL IS HORROR STRUCK. (Original 1888 Book Image)

CROOKS OF THE EAST END, WHITECHAPEL, LONDON. (Original 1888 Book Image)

ILLUSTRATED POLICE NEWS, SEPTEMBER 8TH 1888.

29 HANBURY STREET IN AUGUST, 1967.

SKETCH OF REAR YARD, 29 HANBURY ST.

PHOTOGRAPH OF REAR YARD, 29 HANBURY ST.

OLD MONTAGUE STREET IN 1961

ANNIE CHAPMAN (Annie Sievy)

POLICE NEWS, SEPTEMBER 17, 1888

ARREST BY THE POLICE ON SUSPICION. (Original 1888 Book Image)

DISCOVERY OF BODY IN BERNERS STREET.

DISCOVERY OF BODY IN MITRE SQUARE.

MITRE SQUARE. BODY WAS DISCOVERED IN FRONT OF GATE.

CATHARINE EDDOWES MORTUARY PHOTOGRAPH.

NEWSPAPER REPORT OF THE DOUBLE MURDER.

THE RATCLIFFE HIGHWAY MURDERS

AN UNFORUNATE IN WHITECHAPLE GIVING HER LOVER MONEY. (Original 1888 Book Image)

DISCOVERING A BODY. (Original 1888 Book Image)

NEWSPAPER ILLUSTRATION DEPICTING THE ESCAPE OF JOHN TURNER FROM THE SECOND FLOOR OF THE KING'S ARMS AFTER HE DISCOVERED THE SECOND MURDERS, DECEMBER 1811.

PROCESSION TO INTERMENT OF JOHN WILLIAMS (MURPHY) THE WRETCHED SUICIDE AND REPUTED MURDERER OF THE MARRS AND WILLIAMSONS FAMILIES WHO HANGED HIMSELF AND WAS BURIED IN A FOUR WENT WAY CANNON STREET RATCLIFF ON DEC 31, 1811 IT IS HERE STOPPING BEFORE THE MURDERED MR WILLIAMSON'S HOUSE.

SKETCH OF JOHN WILLIAMS' CORPSE ON THE DEATH CART, PUBLISHED 4 YEARS AFTER THE EVENT.

WITNESS GIVING TESTIMONY (Original 1888 Book Image)
DETECTIVES DISCOVERING A VICTIM. (Original 1888 Book Image)
DETECTIVES IN WHITECHAPEL DISCUSSING THE SITUATION. (Original 1888 & 1889 Book Image)
AN ABBY ACCOSTING GIRL IN WHITECHAPEL. (Original 1888 Book Image)
DORSET STREET, WHITECHAPEL.
CRISPIN STREET LOOKING TOWARDS SPITALFIELDS MARKET AND DORSET STREET.
ARCHED ENTRENCE TO MILLERS COURT.
MARY KELLY ENTERING HER LODGINGS IN MILLER COURT.
MARY KELLY WITH A STRANGER.
ONE OF THE JACK THE RIPPER REWARD POSTERS.
DISCOVERY OF A VICTIM. (Original 1889 Book Image)
THE FIEND CALMLY SURVEYS HIS BLOODY WORK. (Original 1888 & 1889 Book Image)
BREAKING THE DOOR OPEN
DISCOVERY OF THE MURDER AND THE CROWD THAT SOON GATHERED.

MARY KELLEY'S MUTILATED BODY.
MARY'S ROOM IN MILLER COURT.
A WHITECHAPLE TYPE. (Original 1888 Book Image)
DEAR BOSS, LETTER PAGE 1
DEAR BOSS, LETTER PAGE 2

(1889 VERSION)

INTRODUCTION

CRIME is the transgression, by individuals, of laws made for the protection and good of the community. Every country, civilized and uncivilized, the whole world at large and in all ages has been cursed with crime from Cain the first murderer to the last case reported in the daily newspaper.

For years this country has been flooded with literature professing to be "CHRONICLES OF CRIME" but in reality mere sensational products of the imagination, in plain words the crimes have been manufactured for the occasion.

In these volumes, however, the truth will be strictly adhered to, and every story given can be relied upon as strictly authentic, thus confirming the old maxim, that "*truth is stranger than fiction.*"

(Original 1888 Version)

THE WHITECHAPEL MURDERS

INTRODUCTION

Never in the record of criminal history were the police of any country called upon to unravel a mystery so complete as that which enshrouds the famous murders in Whitechapel, London.

Nine victims have fallen under the skilful knife of an unknown fiend, and there remains not a particle of a clue on which to hang a hope of discovery of the murderer.

From beginning to end the tragedies have been marked by many circumstances and mysterious details which fill all with horror and dismay.

The clubman in his club, the lady in her boudoir, the housewife in her kitchen, the work girl in the shop and factory, the whispering, gin-soaked public woman on the thoroughfare, alike were stirred by these dreadful tidings of heartless and bloody crime.

The Government of Her Majesty was questioned about them in open Parliament.

The Detectives of Scotland Yard put their heads together, plotted, schemed, devised, but all to no purpose.

The ensanguined book of dastardly murder is a sealed book.

One after the other the mutilated victims of this mysterious demon were picked up on the highways of a great city, but no one has seen the murderer, no one suspects who he is, and no one has found him.

A great wave of nervous, feverish alarm and terror swept over the metropolis of Great Britain.

In every case the unmistakable work of the same fiend was too painfully apparent to admit of a doubt that these murders in Whitechapel were wrought by one fell hand.

Madman he probably was, but with all his boldness he possessed a cruel cunning which allowed him to stalk abroad on the public streets, striking down his victims as he pleased, leaving not the faintest clue to his personality.

No conception can be formed of the motives of his horrible crimes, unless it is reasonable to suppose it was the work of a maniac.

Did the fiend experiment on the corpses for anatomical purposes?

Did he seek revenge on the class of public women because of some injury he had himself received from one of them?

Was he a madman—irresponsible, bloodthirsty, craving, supernatural excitements?

These are some of the questions that may resolve themselves when you have read a detailed account of these murders perpetrated in one of the oldest, and, presumably, one of the most civilized cities of the modem world.

WAS A MADMAN PROWLING THE STREETS OF WHITECHAPEL?

CHAPTER I

THE FIRST MURDER

The first of the Whitechapel murder series attracted little public attention. It was perpetrated on April 3rd, 1888. The victim was Emma Elizabeth Smith.

As the policeman stooped over her, looked into her bloodless face, in the light of bulls-eye lantern, gazed into her blear eyes, smelt her gin-soaked breath, examined her bloodstained clothes, he reported the case to headquarters.

The officials did not bother much about it.

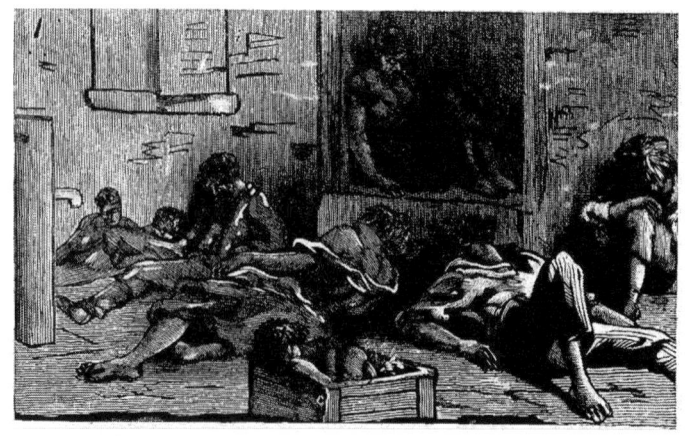

HOW THEY LIVED IN WHITECHAPEL
(Original 1888 Book Image)

Only a woman of the lowest class, they thought, murdered in a drunken brawl.

What else can you expect in Whitechapel with its floating population of criminals and fallen women?

The press commented a little on the incident; the clubman yawned after he read about it at his supper; the fine lady remarked it was shocking as she buttered her muffins at breakfast, and then the disagreeable subject was dismissed.

> *Rattle her bones*
> *Over the stones,*
> *She's only a pauper*
> *Whom nobody owns.*

(Above Rhyme appeared in the original 1888 version)

CHAPTER II

THE SECOND MURDER

Martha Turner was a poor hawker in Whitechapel.

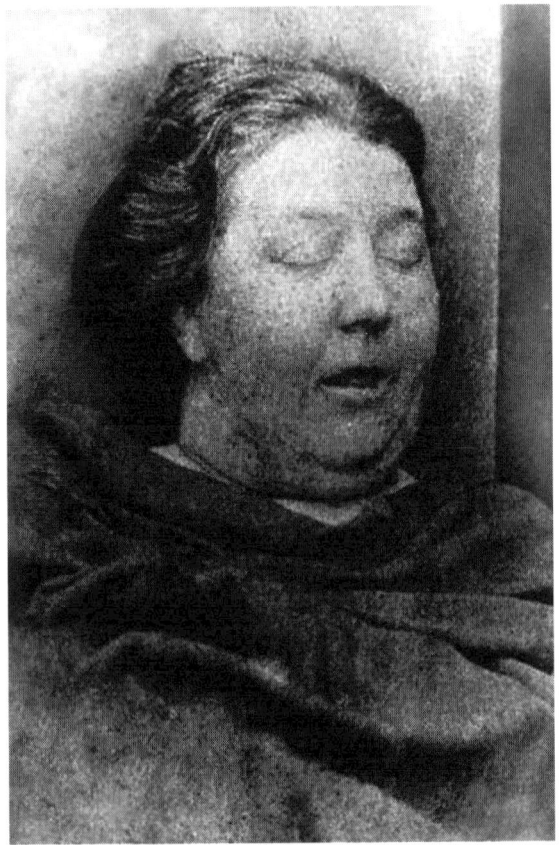

MARTHA TURNER (OR MARTHA TABRAM)

On Tuesday, August 7, 1888, this Martha Turner was found lying on her back, her clothing disarrayed, on the first floor landing of the buildings known as George Yard Buildings, Commercial Street, Spitalfields, Whitechapel.

Her throat was cut, her breasts were amputated and lay beside her, her legs were lacerated with knife gashes, and the blood stained the floor with clotted red.

The day previous to the second murder had been what is known as '*Bank Holiday*' and it was late in the evening that day that the murder had been perpetrated.

Martha Turner had evidently met her fate by the same hand that struck down Emma Elizabeth Smith.

The same mutilation of the same parts was visible.

The same rapid work was traceable in the assassin's onslaught.

As nearly as the police could determine, both women had been seized suddenly, unexpectedly by a powerful arm from behind, and their throats cut swiftly by the rapid stroke of a razor-edged knife.

Such was the force of the murderer's death blow, and such the keenness of his devilish weapon, that the head was almost severed from the body and hung loose. The knife had left its imprint upon the bone at the back of the neck.

But more remarkable than the ghastly work at the throat, was the discovery that the woman had received no less than thirty-nine distinct deep and clear cut stabs upon various parts of her body.

From these wounds the blood had poured forth, saturating her clothes and covering the steps on which she lay with a slippery coating of coagulated blood.

Examination of the body revealed the same horrible, indescribable mutilation of the uterus that had marked the first murder.

The underclothing of coarse material had been thrown roughly up over the victim's head and a jagged wound crossed the bowels, laying bare the intestines.

Below this a portion of the woman's body had been cut out with the nicety and skill of a surgeon's knife, leaving only a blood-oozing and quivering aperture.

The organ had been removed as in the case of the first murder.

Horror seized the police authorities on seeing this sight.

Several friends of the victim were arrested and held by the coroner.

But little was found that cast light on the crime.

A WHITECHAPLE TYPE (Original 1888 Book Image)

At the inquest, Mary Ann Connelly, known in Whitechapel as *'Pearly Poll,'* was a witness, who was expected to give valuable information.

Inspector Reid asked that she might be cautioned prior to being sworn, and the coroner complied with his request.

"I am a single woman," testified *'Pearly Poll.'* " I've been lodging in a lodging house in Dorset Street. I've gained my livelihood on the streets. I've known the murdered woman for four or five months. We called her *'Emma.'* The last time I saw her alive was on Bank Holiday, at the corner of George Yard, Whitechapel. We went to a public house together and parted at 11.45. We were accompanied by two soldiers, one a private and one a corporal. I don't know to what regiment they belonged, but they had white bands around their caps. I don't remember whether the corporal had side arms or not. We picked up with the soldiers together and entered several public houses. We drank in each of the houses.

When we separated, '*Emma*' went away with the private. They went up to George Yard and I and my fellow went to Angel Alley. Before I went away from my fellow I had a quarrel, and he hit me with a stick. I didn't hear '*Emma*' have a quarrel. I never saw her alive again.

'*Emma*' wasn't given to drink. I tried to pick out the two men who were with us. I tried at Wellington Barracks. The men were paraded before me; but though I saw two men something like those who were with us on the night of the murder, I couldn't be sure. I left my fellow, the corporal, at five or ten minutes past 12 that morning, and afterwards went along Commercial Street towards Whitechapel. I didn't hear no screams. I didn't hear of the murder till Tuesday."

'Pearly Poll' was the only witness who could give any news at all about Martha Turner, and that news, as you see, was scant enough.

The authorities were baffled.

The public was beginning to be aroused.

CHAPTER III

THE THIRD MURDER

Scarcely had aristocratic West End of London recovered from the second murder in low-life East End when the city and the world were cast into new spasms by the flash of news that a third crime had been committed in the cursed, crime-stained precincts of Whitechapel.

Everybody asked: "Who is it?"

And the answer came swifter than death: "Another woman!"

This time it was Mary Ann Nichols, aged forty-two, a woman of the lowest class. She had been killed and mutilated.

Her body was found in the street in Buck's Row, Whitechapel, in the early morning of Friday, August 31.

DISCOVERY OF BODY IN BUCKS ROW.

Mary Ann Nichols had evidently not been killed on the spot where her body lay dead.

She had evidently been killed at another spot and dragged to where she lay.

There was little blood around the corpse.

Buck's Row is a short street, half occupied by factories, half by dwelling houses.

Half down this street is the house of Mrs. Green.

Next to this house is a large stable yard, whose wide, closed gateway is next to the house.

In front of the gateway, Mary Ann Nicholls was found.

The brutality of the murder is beyond conception and beyond description.

The throat was cut in two gashes, the instrument of crime having been a sharp one, but used in a most ferocious and reckless way.

There was a gash under the left ear, reaching nearly to the centre of the throat.

Along half its length, however, it was accompanied by another one, which reached around under the other ear, making a wide and horrible hole and nearly severing the head from the body.

No murder was ever more ferociously or more brutally done.

The knife, which must have been a large and sharp one, was jabbed into the deceased at the lower part of the abdomen, and then drawn upward twice.

A sickening sight, truly, such as unmanned the most hardened official.

DISCOVERY OF A VICTIM.
(Original 1888 Book Image)

ALL WHITECHAPEL IS HORROR STRUCK.
(Original 1888 Book Image)

CROOKS OF THE EAST END, WHITECHAPEL LONDON.
(Original 1888 Book Image)

Constable O'Neill, who discovered the lifeless body, immediately rapped at the house of Mrs. Green.

"Have you heard any unusual noise?" he asked, wiping the perspiration from his brow.

Then he pointed out the body.

Mrs. Green almost fainted when she saw the ghastly spectacle.

Constable O'Neill put his hand on the woman's shoulder and repeated the question.

Mrs. Green, as though demented, shook her head in the negative.

Then Constable O'Neill questioned the son and daughter of Mrs. Green.

"We have heard no outcry," said they.

"The night was unusually quiet," said Mrs. Green, finally.

"I should have heard a noise, if there had been any, for I have trouble with my heart, and am a very light sleeper."

Then Constable O'Neill questioned Mr. Perkins, an opposite neighbour to the Greens' but he also denied having heard a noise in the still air of night.

Several people, however, remembered strange sounds.

"I was awakened Friday morning," testified Mrs. Perkins, a neighbour, "by my little girl, who said someone was trying to get into the house.

I listened and heard screams. They were in a woman's voice, and though frightened, were faint-like, as would be natural if she was running. She was screaming, "*Murder! Police! Murder!*" She seemed to be all alone. I think I would have heard the steps if anybody had been running after her, unless he were running on tip-toe."

The detectives of Scotland Yard, thoroughly aroused by this third murder, at once searched everywhere in the vicinity, in the hope of discovering some clue.

None was found.

Everything pointed to the fact that the murder was committed at some distance from where the body lay.

There were drops of blood all along the sidewalks.

But there was a mystery even here.

The police were puzzled by the fact that there were blood stains on both sides of the street.

Amid a gaping, terror-stricken crowd, the blood-clotted body of Mary Ann Nichols was lifted on a stretcher and conveyed to the death house.

A cordon of police had to keep the crowd back.

It took some time to identify her positively.

The clothing wore a workhouse stamp. A comb and a piece of looking glass were found in one of the pockets.

Finally, four women identified her, said they knew her by the name of '*Polly*.'

"We have lived with her at 18 Thrawl Street, Spitalfields," said they. "We lived there in a room. We paid four pence a night."

On the night of the murder, it appears Mary Ann Nichols, alias 'Polly,' was turned out of this house because she hadn't money to pay for her lodgings.

She was then a little the worse for drink and said, as she was turned away:

"I'll soon get my 'doss' money. See what a jolly bonnet I've got now!"

The lodging house people only knew her as 'Polly,' but later a woman from Lambeth Workhouse identified her as Mary Ann Nichols.

The deceased woman had been an inmate of the workhouse and left it to take a situation as a servant, but after a short time she absconded with £3 of her employer's money.

From that time forth she was an outcast.

The police theory was at that time that a sort of '*high rip*' gang existed in the neighbourhood, which, blackmailing women of the 'unfortunate' class, takes vengeance on those who do not find money for them.

They base that surmise on the fact that within twelve months two other women have been murdered in the district by almost similar means—one as recently as the 6th of August last—and left in the gutter of the street in the early hours of the morning.

At the coroner's inquest, no testimony was adduced that tended to cast any light on the horrible mystery.

The deceased woman's husband, who is a printer's machinist, testified that he had lived apart from his wife for over eight years, and the last time he saw her alive was three years ago. His wife had left him of her own accord, and her drinking habits had led her into a dissolute life.

ILLUSTRATED POLICE NEWS, SEPTEMBER 8TH 1888.

CHAPTER IV

THE FOURTH MURDER

A week after the killing of Mary Ann Nicholls, another fallen woman—Annie Chapman, aged forty-five—was found killed and hacked like the rest, this making the fourth murder.

Her body was discovered in Buck's Row, Whitechapel. [*Mistake by author. Nicholls was found in Bucks Row, not Chapman.*]

John Davies, living on top floor of 29 Hanbury Street, stumbled across it on the morning of Friday, August 31, and yelled for the police.

29 HANBURY STREET IN AUGUST, 1967.

At a spot a very few hundred yards from where the mangled body of the poor woman, Nichols, was found just a week before lay this body of another woman, mutilated and horribly disfigured.

She was found at 5.30 on Sunday morning, lying in the back yard of No. 20 Hanbury Street, Spitalfields. A house occupied by Mr. Richardson, a packing-case maker. As late as 5 o'clock on Saturday morning, it is said, the woman was drinking in a public house near at hand, called the Ten Bells.

SKETCH OF REAR YARD, 29 HANBURY ST.

Near the body was discovered a rough piece of iron sharpened like a knife. The wounds upon the poor woman were more fearful than those found upon the body of the woman Nichols, who was buried on Thursday. The throat was cut in a most horrible manner, and the stomach terribly mutilated.

The bowels were ripped open.

The intestines hung out.

The place was a pool of blood.

While Davies cried for the police, Mrs. Richardson, an old lady sleeping on the first floor front, was aroused by her grandson, Charles Cooksley, who looked out of one of the back windows and screamed that there was a dead body in the corner.

Mrs. Richardson's description makes this murder even more horrible than any of its predecessors.

The victim was lying on her back, with her legs outstretched.

Her throat was cut from ear to ear. Her clothes were pushed up above her waist and her legs bare. The abdomen was exposed, the woman having been ripped up from groin to breast-bone, as in the preceding cases. Not only this, but the viscera had been pulled out and scattered in all directions, the heart and liver being placed behind her head and the remainder along her side. No more horrible sight ever met a human eye, for she was covered with blood and lying in a pool of it.

The throat was cut open in a fearful manner—so deep, in fact, that the murderer, evidently thinking that he had severed the head from the body, tied a handkerchief round it so as to keep it on. There was no blood on the clothes. Hanbury Street is a long street which runs from Baker's Row to Commercial Street. It consists partly of shops and partly of private houses. In the house in question, in the front room on the ground floor, Mr. Harderman carries on the business of a seller of cats meat. At the back of the premises are those of Mr. Richardson, who is a packing case maker. The other occupants of the house are lodgers. One of the lodgers, named Robert Thompson, who is a car-man, went out of the house at 3.30 in the morning, but heard no noise. Two girls, who also live in the house, were talking in the passage until 12.30 with young men, and it is believed that they were the last occupants of the house to retire to rest.

PHOTOGRAPH OF REAR YARD, 29 HANBURY ST.

It seems that the crime was committed soon after 5. At that hour the woman and the man, who in all probability was her murderer, were seen drinking together in the Bells, Brick Lane.

But though the murder was committed at this late hour, the murderer—acting, as in the other case, silently and stealthily—managed to make his escape.

On the wall near where the body was found, there was, according to one reporter, discovered written in chalk:

FIVE: 15 MORE AND THEN I GIVE MYSELF UP.

Jack the Ripper.

Davies, the lodger, who discovered the body, immediately communicated with the police at the Commercial Street station, and Inspector Chandler and several constables arrived on the scene in a short time, when they found the woman in the condition described.

An excited crowd gathered in front of Mrs. Richardson's house, and also around the mortuary in Old Montague Street, to which place the body was quickly removed.

Several persons who were lodging in the house, and who were seen in the vicinity when the body was found, were taken to the Commercial Street station and closely examined, especially the women last with the deceased.

OLD MONTAGUE STREET IN 1961

Inquiries led to the discovery that the woman was known by several names. Her real name was Annie Chapman, but she had latterly passed as Annie Sievy, and rejoiced in the nickname of *'Dark Annie.'*

Her age was about forty-five. She was 6 feet high, had fair, brown, wavy hair, blue eyes, and, like Mary Ann Nicholls, had two teeth missing. One peculiarity of her features was a large, flat kind of nose. Her clothing was old and dirty, and nothing was found in her pockets except part of envelope bearing the seal of the Sussex Regiment.

For the last nine months she had been sleeping at a lodging-house, 35 Dorset Street, Spitalfields, and she was there as recently as 2 o'clock on Saturday morning eating some potatoes. She had not, however, the money to pay for her bed, and at 2 o'clock she left with the remark to the keeper of the place:

"I'll soon be back again ; I'll soon get the money for my doss."

Almost the very words Mary Ann Nicholls used to the companion she met in Whitechapel Road, at 2.30 on the morning of her death.

A companion identified her soon after she had been taken to the mortuary as '*Dark Annie*,' and as she came from the mortuary gate, bitterly crying, said between her tears:

"I knowed her; I kissed her poor, cold face."

The large, flat kind of nose of the deceased was so striking a peculiarity that the police hoped to be able to fully trace the movements of the deceased by means of it. The clothing of the dead woman, like that of most of her class who ply their trade in this quarter of London, was old and dirty.

In the dress of the dead woman, two farthings were found, so brightly polished as to lead to the belief that they were intended to be passed as half-sovereigns, and it is probable that they were given to her by the murderer as an inducement for her to accompany him.

Late on Saturday, after the deceased had been formally identified as Annie Sievy, a witness came forward and stated that her real name was Annie Chapman. She came from Windsor and had friends residing at Vauxhall. She had been married, her husband being an army pensioner, who had allowed her 10 shillings a week, but he died twelve month ago, and the pension ceasing, she became one of the hideous women infesting Whitechapel. She lived for a time with a sieve-maker in Dorset Street, and was known to her acquaintances as '*Annie Sievy*,' a nickname derived from her paramour's trade.

Mrs. Fiddymont, wife of the proprietor of the Prince Albert public house, better known as the *'Clean House,'* at the corner of Brushfield and Stewart Streets, half a mile from the scene of the murder, told the police that at 7 o'clock on Saturday morning she was standing in the bar talking with another woman, a friend, in the first compartment.

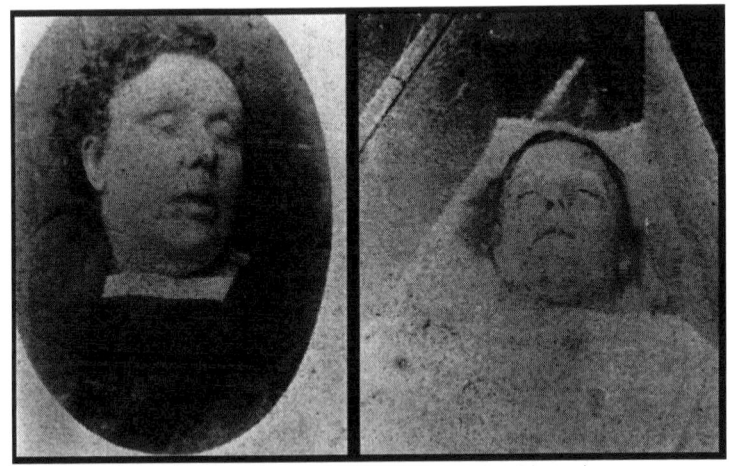

ANNIE CHAPMAN (Annie Sievy)

Suddenly came into the middle compartment a man whose rough appearance frightened her. He had a brown stiff hat, a dark coat and no waistcoat. He came in with his hat down over his eyes, and with his face partly concealed, asked for a half pint of ale. She drew the ale, and meanwhile looked at him through the mirror at the back of the bar.

As soon as he saw the woman in the other compartment watching him, he turned his back, and put the partition between himself and her. The thing that struck Mrs. Fiddymont particularly was the fact that there were blood spots on the back of his right hand.

This, taken in connection with his appearance, caused her uneasiness. She also noticed that his shirt was torn. As soon as he had drank the ale, which he swallowed at a gulp, he went out.

Her friend went out also to watch the man.

Her friend was Mary Chappell, who lives at No. 28 Stewart Street, nearby. Her story corroborates Mrs. Fiddymont's. When the man came in, the expression of his eyes caught her attention, his look was so startling and terrifying.

It frightened Mrs. Fiddymont so that she requested her to stay. He wore a light blue check shirt, which was torn badly—into rags, in fact—on the right shoulder.

There was a narrow streak of blood under his right ear, parallel with the edge of his shirt. There was also dried blood between the fingers of his hand. When he went out, she slipped out the other door and watched him as he went toward Bishopsgate Street. She called Joseph Taylor's attention to him, and he followed him.

Taylor is a builder, at No. 22 Stewart Street, and said that as soon as his attention was attracted to the man he followed him.

He walked rapidly and came alongside of him, but did not speak to him. The man was rather thin, about 5 feet 8 inches high and apparently between forty and fifty years of age.

He had a shabby-genteel look, pepper-and-salt trousers, which fitted badly, and dark coat. When Taylor came alongside of him, the man glanced at him, and Taylor's description of the look was, "*His eyes were as wild as a hawk's.*"

Was this man with the sharp eye also the man with the sharp knife?

Was he the Whitechapel murderer?

Time, perhaps, will tell.

CHAPTER V

THE FIFTH MURDER

'*Jack, the Ripper*,' had got to be a thing of flesh and blood in the households of England.

The man of Whitechapel inspired the fear once inspired by Guy Fawkes.

Mothers hushed their unruly children by saying:

"Be quiet, or '*Jack, the Ripper*,' will come."

The police were still at work.

The officials of Scotland Yard were more than usually busy.

A cordon of constables surrounded Whitechapel.

Bloodhounds were called into use, and sniffed the dirty pavements.

The women of the quarter did without food and drink—dared not venture into the streets.

Every man they saw seemed to them the demon.

Every man loomed up as '*Jack, the Ripper,*' the fiend who would be satisfied with no less than fifteen victims.

POLICE NEWS, SEPTEMBER 17, 1888

It was on Sunday. September 23—a calm, quiet, autumnal day of rest.

The churches and cathedrals of England were full of devout worshippers.

Suddenly there flashed across the wires that a murder had been committed at Gateshead, near Newcastle-on-Tyne, in the North of England.

Again, a feeling of apprehension seized all classes.

A young woman—disembowelled, mangled, mutilated, unrecognizable—lay cold in death on the roadside.

Who did the dastardly deed?

Everything pointed to the conclusion that this murder at Gateshead was the fell stroke of *'Jack, the Ripper,'* of Whitechapel. His fifth murder.

The epidemic of fear in London now became more horrible than before.

The most callous elegants of the West End now became thoroughly alarmed.

But *'Jack, the Ripper,'* merely grinned with fiendish glee, and kept from the sleuthhounds of the public. He hadn't killed his fifteen yet.

ARREST BY THE POLICE ON SUSPICION.
(Original 1888 Book Image)

CHAPTER VI

THE SIXTH AND SEVENTH VICTIMS

On the night of September 30, the streets of London were echoing with shrieks of murder.

Two more unfortunate women had been added to the list of the butchered in Whitechapel, being the sixth and seventh victims.

Elizabeth Stride, nicknamed '*Hippy Lip Anny*,' forty years of age, was found murdered in Berners Street at 1 o'clock in the morning. Her throat was cut, but there was no slashing of the remains.

The body was warm when found, and the murderer had evidently been frightened away.

DISCOVERY OF BODY IN BERNER STREET.

Now, fifteen minutes after the discovery of the dead body of '*Hippy Lip Anny*,' the mutilated body of another victim—a degraded woman of the Whitechapel district, named Catharine Eddowes—was found in the north-west corner of Mitre Square.

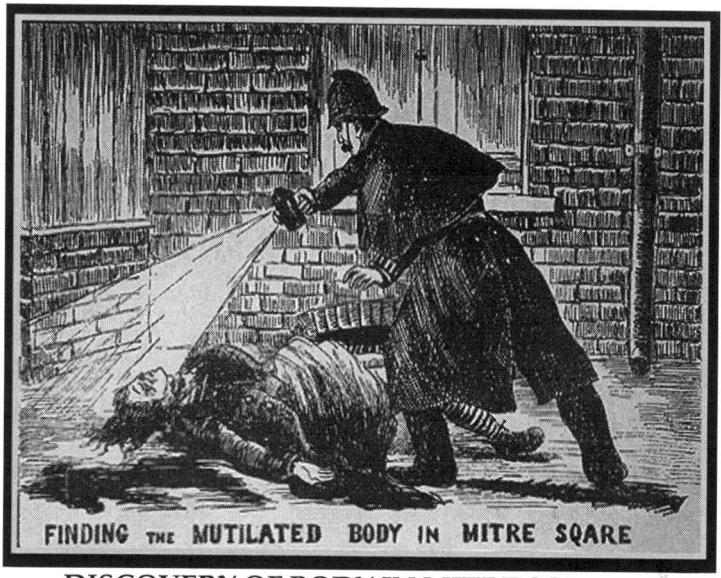

DISCOVERY OF BODY IN MITRE SQUARE.

The older portion of London abounds with these cul-de-sacs, inaccessible to wagons, and to be reached only by footpaths through private property. A stranger in London would never think of entering one of them, but the old Londoner knows them well as convenient short cuts.

There are two street lamps in Mitre Square, and they were burning brightly at 1 o'clock this morning.

A large tea house in the square hires a private watchman, and. he was on duty last night, with lights blazing from five windows.

He is a veteran policeman, and looks like a wide-awake, trustworthy man. Less than two hundred feet from the tea house are three or four dwelling houses, with bedroom windows facing the square, and at least twenty people sleeping in them.

MITRE SQUARE. BODY WAS DISCOVERED IN FRONT OF GATE

The policeman on the beat goes through the square every fifteen minutes throughout the night, searching corners with a dark lantern and rousing out homeless people who fall asleep on the area railings. The policeman who was on the beat at 1 o'clock this morning was a stalwart, honest looking fellow.

At 1.30 this morning he passed through the square, searching all corners with his lantern and stopping for at least half a minute in one particular corner right under the bedroom windows of a dwelling-house. Everything was silent and dark, except the windows of the tea-house, where the watchman was awake, reading.

Fifteen minutes afterward, the policeman passed the same corner again. This time he found a woman stretched dead upon the pavement in a pool of blood, her throat cut, her nose torn from the face, the clothes thrown back over the body, the abdomen gashed into pieces and the intestines wrenched from the stomach.

The policeman started.

He ran over to the tea-house and hammered on the door.

"What's the matter?" shouted the watchman.

"For God's sake," said the policeman, "come out and assist me! Another woman has been ripped open."

Not a sound had the watchman heard. The slumbers of the people in the dwelling-houses had not been disturbed. Within fifteen minutes a merciless murder had been committed, and the murderer had disappeared in the darkness without the slightest clue for the police to follow.

It was a horrible sight. Every sweep of the assassin's knife had been made to tell. It was a woman about forty-five years old, poorly nourished, shabbily dressed, undoubtedly an unfortunate who picked up a living on the streets. In this case no organs were missing, as in the bodies of the women previously murdered. The cuts on the stomach were almost in the shape of the letter T, the upward cut stretching from the uterus to the breast and the crosscut slanting from the lower part of the left ribs to the right hip.

The deed must have been done with a heavy knife, and by someone skilled in the use of it—no jagged hacking, but clean cuts, scientifically made.

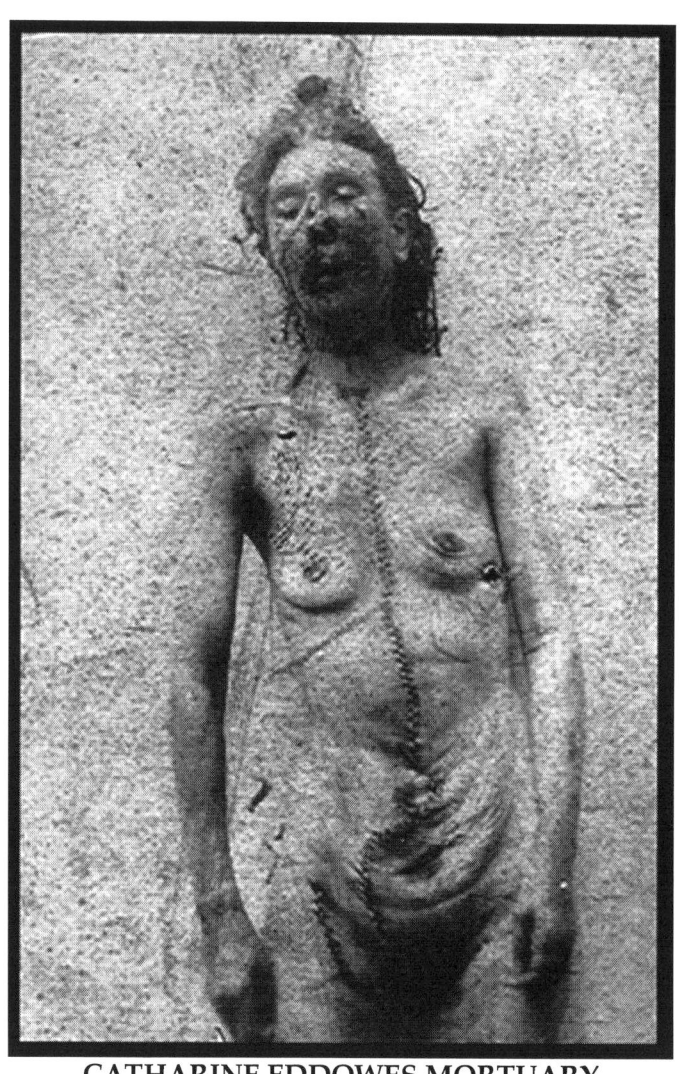

CATHARINE EDDOWES MORTUARY PHOTOGRAPH.

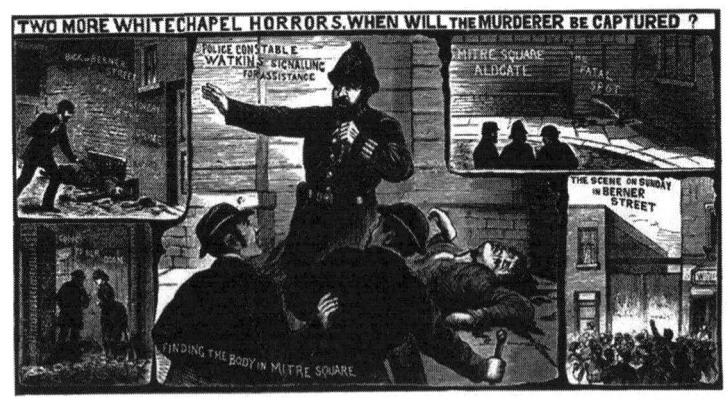

NEWSPAPER REPORT OF THE DOUBLE MURDER.

Several doctors arrived and examined the body. They found a prodigious quantity of blood, which had flowed chiefly from the throat, but the murderer had so carefully avoided it that not a single footmark could be traced. The body was removed to the mortuary, where a careful post-mortem examination took place.

There was a tattoo mark of a figure '*4*' on the woman's left forearm.

Throngs of noisy men, dissolute women and squalid children surrounded the localities where the murders were committed and the places where the bodies await the coroner.

They struggled and fought with each other to gain admittance to the dead-house and the police had to use brute force to drive them back. It was a panic of fear and frenzy that those who witnessed will never forget.

Early in the day, people were allowed in the dead-house to see the woman found on Berner Street and to try and identify her.

As soon as she was identified, the doors were closed to all except persons having business there.

Those living in the neighbourhood who did get a chance to approach the corpse paraded the streets all day with bloodstains of the victim on their fingers and described the appearance of the body over and over again to all the people who would listen to them.

CHAPTER VII

THE EIGHTH MURDER

London was now thoroughly alarmed.

Sir Charles Warren issued a proclamation.

The Lord Mayor offered a big reward for the capture of the murderer.

Even the swell in the West End stopped sucking the end of his cane and showed considerable animation over the horror, which took place with such startling successive rapidity.

Everybody felt that the condition of the lost women in London ought to be investigated.

(The following text is original to the 1888 version)

Girls in Whitechapel did as well as they could.

They were debarred from other callings by adverse circumstances.

Take the case of Catherine Harris, a tall, light-haired woman, known at the West End as a vender of flowers, read her testimony in court, and see how hard it is for girls to get along in the metropolis nowadays.

The scene took place in the Marlborough Street Police Court.

Catherine Harris was arraigned, charged with begging in Piccadilly.

Here is the account of her trial:

Catherine Harris, the prisoner, brought into court a small basket, containing flowers, but it was taken from her and placed at her feet. Constable 339 C said that at twenty minutes past twelve o'clock on Sunday morning, he saw the prisoner accost two gentlemen and ask them to buy her '*pretty flowers.*' They refused to purchase any, and then she asked for sixpence for her night's lodgings. She persisted in her request; but finding that they paid no heed to her she proceeded to the corner of the Circus, and there interrogated other gentlemen in a similar manner, telling them that she had been out all night, and had only taken two pence.

Mr. Hannay: Do you wish to ask any questions?

The Prisoner: Well, sir, I bought two dozen of pretty flowers on Saturday, and just look at them now. (Laughter.) Look at them violets, tuber-colour roses, and Chinese asters just look at them and see what these wretches of police have done to them. (Laughter.) They put me into a cell and my pretty flowers into a pail of dirty water. (Laughter.)I have been selling flowers for many years and, Mr. Mansfield at one time sent me to a workhouse, but they would not take me in, saying that I was to go to my parish in Bristol. I am not a thief or anything of that kind.

Mr. Hannay: You are charged with begging.

Prisoner: Begging, indeed; I did not beg. I wanted to sell my pretty flowers. If they (the police) see me speak to a gentleman, they swear that am begging. I got up at five o'clock on Saturday morning and bought my flowers in Covent Garden, and that's what I call getting an honest living. I came into Piccadilly because I can get a better price there than can get in the Strand. In Piccadilly a swell or a gay woman will give me sixpence for a pretty flower, but in the Strand the poor devils can only afford twopence or threepence. The police persecute me more than they do the man who committed all those murders he is not persecuted half so much as I am. I assure you the police will swear black is white. (Laughter.)

Mr. Hannay: The constable says that you begged of the gentlemen after they refused to buy your flowers.

Prisoner: Oh, no; I never beg.

Sergeant Brewer said that prisoner had been several times in the dock, charged with disorderly conduct or begging.

Prisoner (loudly:) Well, I've not been here for robbery, have I?

(Laughter.) It's a nice thing to laugh at.

Mr. Hannay: Ten days.

Prisoner: Here, give me my flowers. What a nerve! (more laughter) and the woman and her *'pretty flowers'* disappeared from the dock.

This throws some light on the state of things in fashionable West End

(End of 1888 text)

AN UNFORUNATE IN WHITECHAPLE GIVING HER LOVER MONEY.
(Original 1888 Book Image)

DISCOVERING A BODY.
(Original 1888 Book Image)

Is it a wonder there are so many degraded women in London?

If West End is full of iniquity and injustice, can you marvel at dissipation and debauch in East End?

London was soon stirred by another sensation.

THE RATCLIFFE HIGHWAY MURDERS

On October 2, 1888, the highly decomposed remains of a woman were found on the site of the projected Metropolitan Opera House, on the Thames Embankment.

The spot is near Charing Cross, three miles west of Whitechapel.

But the state of the body, the gashes, the mutilations, the cuts, the holes in the flesh, proved plainly that the murderer was the old fiend; that this was his eighth victim.

He had evidently attacked his victim from behind, cut her throat from ear to ear, dug his knife into her breasts.

Then he had raised her poor, dishevelled clothing, slit the body right and left, and left the intestines exposed in a clotted pool of blood.

There had evidently been a hard fight.

Spots of gore were spattered all over the pavement.

But the victim, in spite of her struggles, had succumbed to the hellish adroitness and diabolical strength of her foul assailant.

There she lay in the moonlight—stiff, stark dead.

And the murderer escaped.

Newsboys hawked about the dreadful news.

London at its breakfast read of a new tragedy.

The calls for the resignation of Sir Charles Warren, Chief of Metropolitan Police, already loud, grow louder.

Old men told the story of crimes in the olden times.

Terrible as this eighth murder was, Whitechapel had been the scene of mysterious murders before.

Close upon eighty years since it, and, indeed, the whole country, was startled by the perpetration of a series of most revolting murders, the scene being Ratcliffe Highway. The malefactor, whoever he was—for it was never definitely decided, although there was a case of strong circumstantial evidence, almost amounting to certainty, against an Irish sailor named Williams or Murphy—did not, in these instances, seek out and mark down unfortunate women of the lowest class, but looked for his victims in the persons of respectable trades-people and their families, slaughtered without mercy every human being within the four walls, sparing not even the defenceless, innocent babe in the cradle.

The two distinct crimes, in which seven lives were taken, occurred within the space of a fortnight. The first, the murder of the whole household of the Marrs, at No. 29 Ratcliffe Highway, soon after midnight of Saturday, December 8, 1811, and the second, a similar massacre of the Williamsons, at No. 81 New Gravel Lane, Ratcliffe Highway, between eleven and twelve o'clock on the night of the 19th of the same month.

In the first case four persons in all were the victims of the outrage. They were Mr. and Mrs. Marr, each of whom were under twenty-five years of age, their infant, four months old, and James Gohen, the apprentice, fourteen years of age. The servant girl would doubtless have shared the same fate but that she had been sent out on an errand, and on her return, having been absent less than twenty minutes, she found the house in darkness, and subsequently the bodies were discovered lying in various parts of the ground floor and upon the staircase.

Three persons perished in the second case. They were Mr. and Mrs. Williamson, the landlord and landlady of the King's Arms, and their maid-servant, who was found in like manner at the bottom front of the house.

A delirium and panic seized Londoners in general, and those living in the East End especially, as had seldom or never been known before. People barricaded their doors and windows as if in momentary expectation of a siege, and there were some who even died of fright as they heard their shutters or doors tried by persons who, at the worst, were probably meditating nothing more serious than burglary.

Nor was the alarm confined to the metropolis. A notion had somehow got abroad that the murderer, whoever he was, had left London, and a state of the wildest terror prevailed all over the country. It is an ill wind that blows nobody good, and those were fine times for locksmiths, ironmongers, carpenters and the like. Everybody was having new shutters, doors, bolts, bars and locks. Indeed, the door-chain, which upon old doors is so often of tremendous strength and weight, owes its origin to the prevailing alarm which existed. For many months afterward he would be in truth a bold, and, his neighbours would say, a rash man who answered a knock at the door or a ring at the bell before peering cautiously through the slit which the chain permitted. Even the caricaturists of the day, ready enough as a rule to seize hold of anything which excited the public mind, seemed to have been too frightened to make capital out of the murders, and the political cartoons which introduced hammers and razors, the instruments with which the crimes were committed, are but one or two.

(The following text is original to the 1888 version)

But, as may be readily imagined, the broad-sheet mongers were to the fore with some such doggerel as this:

> *"Cease your worldly cares to mind, now,*
> *Since your life it is not long,*
> *And a moment, with attention,*
> *Listen to my mournful song;*
> *While I tell a shocking story,*
> *Which of late has happened here,*
> *Enough to fill the soul with horror,*
> *And to melt your hearts with fear"*

(End of 1888 text)

Then, as now, in this particular district, the shopkeepers were in the habit of keeping open until midnight, and later on Saturday, and Mr. Marr, who is described as a '*man mercer*,' or a hosier, as the modern term has it, at a few minutes before twelve, his shop being still open, gave his servant, Margaret Jewell, a £1 note, instructing her to pay the baker's bill and to bring in some oysters, which was no doubt a Saturday night, or Sunday morning, to be more accurate, a treat after the labours of the week.

WITNESS GIVING TESTIMONY.
(Original 1888 Book Image)

Margaret went to the Baker's, and, finding it shut, returned past the shop, which was yet open, and her master was still behind the counter. She then went to get the oysters; but, finding the shop shut up also, returned, after an absence of twenty minutes in all, finding the shop closed and everything in darkness.

Upon knocking she was unable to gain admittance. Presently, a watchman passed on the other side of the street with a person in charge, and soon after another watchman came up, calling the hour of one, who told her to move on.

She explained who she was, and the watchman knocked and rang, and then was joined by a neighbour, who got in through the back and opened the door, when they together entered the house. This was the girl's evidence at the inquest, and at this point she fainted away.

A sorry spectacle met their gaze as soon as a light could be procured.

There lay the apprentice upon his face on the staircase with a great hole in his skull where his brains had been knocked out, and with such force had this been done, that portions thereof were bespattered over the walls and ceiling. Mrs. Marr was next found lying on the floor, near the street door, quite dead, her head wounded in a like terrible manner, and Mr. Marr's body without any sign of life, was discovered behind the counter with exactly similar injuries. The only other occupant of the house, an infant four months old, whose innocence had not been sufficient to protect it, was in its cradle, with its throat cut from ear to ear: Its head lay almost severed from its body.

Nothing was missing from the house, although there were £152 in the cash-box, and the ill-fated Marr had nearly £5 in his pockets.

The assassin, whoever he was, had disappeared, leaving behind him a large shipwright mallet, which was covered in blood, weighing two or three pounds, with a handle three feet long, a ripping chisel eighteen inches long, and a wooden mallet about four inches square, with a handle eighteen inches in length.

Mr. Murry, the neighbour, stated that at about ten minutes past twelve he heard a noise in Marr's house like the pushing of a chair, and the watchman said that soon after twelve he had called out that the window was unfastened, and had been answered from within. "*We know it.*"

The girl gave evidence that while she was waiting she heard a child cry, and then someone came downstairs.

Prints of blood-stained footsteps of at least two persons were, it was said, discovered in the rear of the premises, and several people were taken up on suspicion, but were discharged.

The churchwardens of the parish offered a reward of £50, and this was supplemented by £20 from the Thames Police Office, but nothing came of it.

Whilst London was ringing with the news, the terror which already existed was heightened by the intelligence of a crime which was equally barbarous and almost equally inexplicable.

The unfortunate sufferers by the first outrage were buried in the presence of a large number of people on the Sunday following, and on the Thursday after, the twelfth night from their death, the entire household of Williamson's, with one exception, was slaughtered, as already stated.

DETECTIVES DISCOVERING A VICTIM.
(Original 1888 Book Image)

On that night, between eleven and twelve, the passers-by in New Gravel Lane were alarmed by a cry of "*Murder!*" which came from a man, clothed in nothing but his shirt, who was hanging by the sheets of his bed—which he had knotted together—from a second floor window at No. 81 in that thoroughfare. He contrived to reach the ground, and then told those who had hurried up on hearing his cry of "*Murder!*" that murderers were in the house, slaughtering everyone within.

A couple of men thereupon burst open the door, when they found the mistress and maid-servant lying by the kitchen fire with their throats cut from ear to ear. In the cellar was the master of the house also, with his head nearly severed from his body, and one of his legs broken. The grandchild of the murdered man, a little girl, was happily found alive, but there were evidences that the murderer had entered the room, doubtless with the intention of slaying it also, for he was eventually shown pretty clearly to have been the Marr murderer, and, no doubt, his fiendish instincts were equally strong on each occasion. The noise of the breaking door and the persons entering the house, however, prevented his carrying his diabolical purpose into effect.

Rushing upstairs, the crowd found the door of a room locked.

As they burst it open they heard the crash of glass. The murderer had sprung through the window, and in the fog which prevailed was lost to sight.

Then the man in the shirt found an opportunity to speak. It appeared that he was a lodger in the house, and had gone to bed, but was awoke by a cry of "*We shall be murdered!*" Out of bed he sprang, and, looking over the stairs, saw through the window of the taproom a powerful, well-made man, six feet high, dressed in drab, shaggy bearskin coat, stooping over the body of Mrs. Williamson, rifling her pockets. Then upon his terrified ears came the sounds of the sighs of a person in the agonies of death.

Frightened half out of his life, he ran to the top of the house, but could not find the trapdoor whereby to escape. Then he crept back to his room and escaped, as stated, through the window.

Rewards were now offered amounting to £1,500, and a great number of persons were taken up on suspicion. Amongst them was a John Williams or Murphy—for he went by either name—an Irish sailor, lodging at the Pear Tree public-house, not far off.

NEWSPAPER ILLUSTRATION DEPICTING THE ESCAPE OF JOHN TURNER FROM THE SECOND FLOOR OF THE KING'S ARMS AFTER HE DISCOVERED THE SECOND MURDERS, DECEMBER 1811.

The wallet which had been left behind was marked with the initials J. P., and a wallet so marked was missing from tool chest which had been felt at the Pear Tree by John Petersen, a ship's carpenter.

Mr. Vermilee, the landlord, who was at the time of the murders in Newgate for debt, was shown the mallet. Murphy's washerwoman stated that there was blood on a shirt and on some stockings he had sent to her.

More than one person had seen him near Williamson's house on the night of the murder, and others proved that he was well acquainted with both Marr and Williamson.

Then, with that fatal stupidity that so often characterizes the guilty. Murphy, when told on Friday morning of the murder, and, being yet in bed, replied, surlily, "*I know it.*" In his dreams, too, he had muttered words sufficient to implicate him, and so he was apprehended on the same day and committed for trial on the Saturday, a strong escort being provided to guard him on his way to Coldbath Fields Prison. Nor was the caution ill-judged. All along the route he was attended by a howling, roaring mob, anxious to tear him limb from limb, and hurl his quivering flesh to the four winds. Escort and prisoner were only too thankful to get safely to the prison.

PROCESSION TO INTERMENT OF JOHN WILLIAMS (MURPHY) THE WRETCHED SUICIDE AND REPUTED MURDERER OF THE MARRS AND WILLIAMSONS FAMILIES WHO HANGED HIMSELF AND WAS BURIED IN A FOUR WENT WAY CANNON STREET RATCLIFF ON DEC 31, 1811 IT IS HERE STOPPING BEFORE THE MURDERED MR WILLIAMSON'S HOUSE.

Murphy managed, however, to cheat the hangman, and two days after Christmas his lifeless body was discovered hanging by his handkerchief from the iron grating of his cell.

On New Year's Eve Williams's body was removed from the prison at 11 a.m., with "*an immense concourse of persons*", said to total 180,000, taking part in a procession up the Ratcliff Highway. When the cart carrying the body drew opposite the Marrs' house the procession halted for nearly a quarter of an hour. A drawing was made that shows, not the slender man described in newspaper accounts, but a stocky labourer.

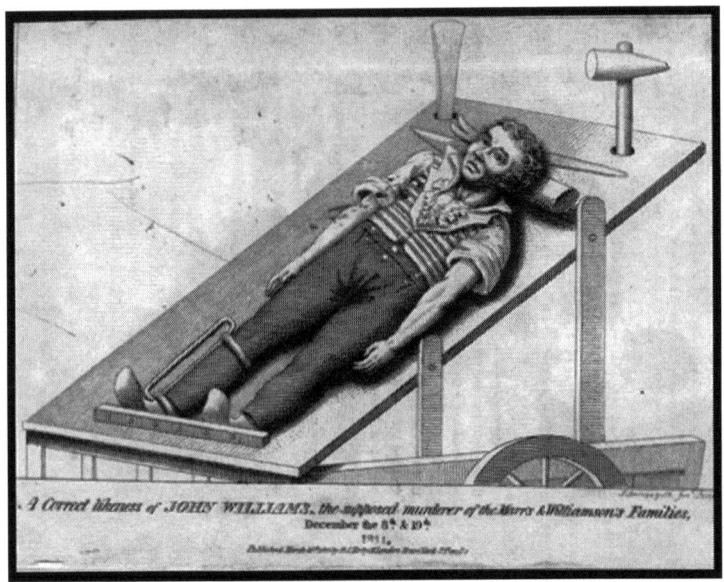

SKETCH OF JOHN WILLIAMS' CORPSE ON THE DEATH CART, PUBLISHED 4 YEARS AFTER THE EVENT.

In his pocket was a piece of metal that he had apparently ripped from the prison wall to stab himself with, in the event that he was unsuccessful at hanging himself.

In accordance with the barbarous custom of the period, the suicide was buried in the dead of night where four roads cross, with a stake driven through his body. Not many months ago Messrs. Aird & Lucas, workmen, in digging a trench for the purpose of laying a main for the Commercial Gas Company at a point where the Cannon Street Road and Cable Street, in St. George's-in-the-East, intersect one another, discovered a skeleton, supposed to be that of Murphy, with a stake driven through it, and some portions of a chain were lying close to the bones.

The death of Murphy did not do much toward allaying the public panic. A general notion prevailed that he had been assisted by accomplices, and two of his friends, named Allbrass and Hart, were apprehended; but after several examinations, they were discharged.

The excitement took a long time to subside, but eventually the occurrences faded out of recollection, and now, with the exception of the journals of the period, there is nothing to keep alive their memory but the innocent door-chain, with which not one in a hundred of the modern jerry-built villas is furnished.

Such is the yam that old people in London tell young people of famous murders in Whitechapel.

Meanwhile, though the old mystery was solved, the new is as deep and dire an enigma as ever.

DETECTIVES IN WHITECHAPEL DISCUSSING THE SITUATION.
(Original 1888 & 1889 Book Image)

AN ABBY ACCOSTING GIRL IN WHITECHAPEL.
(Original 1888 Book Image)

CHAPTER VIII

THE NINTH MURDER

Dorset Street is one of the narrowest, dirtiest little alleys of all those that go to make up the labyrinth known as the East End of London.

To get there a cabman had to ask questions—a rare thing—while his passengers on the journey loses all idea of location, and wonders whether the cab horse's head or tail is pointing toward the north.

DORSET STREET, WHITECHAPEL.

CRISPIN STREET LOOKING TOWARDS SPITALFIELDS MARKET AND DORSET STREET.
(Photograph by C.A. Mathews)

Until today, only a few out of many million landowners knew that Dorset Street in the East End existed, but they know it now, and will, with all other Englishmen, talk about it for weeks.

On the day of the Lord Mayor's Show, November 9, all interest was taken from that senseless pageant by ragged boys struggling through the crowds with bundles of newspapers, and yelling that another horrible Whitechapel murder had occurred in Dorset Street.

You have read about these Whitechapel murders, and you know how the cutting up of some wretched woman is a happening which the average Britisher has come to look for as one of the regular incidents of metropolitan life.

It has got to such a point that those murders can almost be written up after the methodical fashion which characterizes the minutes of some school-board meeting.

Each time a miserable creature belonging to the most degraded class of women is mutilated in a most inconceivably horrible fashion; the murderer has disappeared; the police do nothing but observe secrecy; the general public theorizes as to whether the murderer is mad or sane, short or tall, English or foreign, etc.; the Whitechapel women shiver in bunches, wondering whose turn will come next, and after a while the terror in the East End and the curiosity in the West End subside together until a fresh murder renews them.

The last and ninth Whitechapel murder was not committed in Dorset Street, properly speaking. Out of Dorset Street there opens an arched passage low and narrow.

A big man walking through it would bend his head and turn sideways to keep his shoulders from rubbing against the dirty bricks.

ARCHED ENTRANCE TO MILLERS COURT

At the end of the passage is a high court, not ten feet broad and thirty long, thickly whitewashed all round, for sanitary reasons, to a height of ten feet. That is Miller Court.

Misery is written all over the place—the worst kind of London misery—such as those who have lived their lives in America can have no idea of.

The first door at the end, on the right of the passage, opens into a tiny damp room on a level with the pavement. The landlord of this and neighbouring rooms is a John McCarthy, who keeps a little shop on Dorset Street, on the side of the passage. About a year ago he rented it to a woman who looked about thirty. She was popular among the females of the neighbourhood, who shared her beer generously, as I have been tearfully informed, and went under the title of Mary Jane McCarthy. Her landlord knew that she had another name, Kelly, but her friends had not heard of it.

It seems there had been a Mr. Kelly, whom Mary Jane had married in the manner which is considered satisfactory in Whitechapel.

They had not gone to the expense of a license, but published the fact of matrimony by living in one small room, and sharing joy and sorrow and drunkenness there together.

MARY KELLY ENTERING HER LODGINGS IN MILLER COURT

Mary Jane took up her residence in the little room in Miller Court when Kelly went away.

Since then her life had been that of all the women around her; her drunkenness and the number of strange men she brought to her little room being the gauges by which her sisters in wretchedness measured her prosperity. On November 8 she went out as usual, and was seen at various times up to half past 11 drinking at various low beer shops in Commercial Street.

In those resorts she was known, not as Mary Jane, her own name, but as '*Fair Emma*,' a title bestowed in complimentary allusion to her appearance.

At last, just before midnight, she went home with some man who appears to have dissuaded her from making a good-night visit, as was her custom, at the drinking place nearest her room.

No description whatever can be obtained of this man.

Right opposite the passage leading to Mary Jane's room is a big and very pretentious lodging-house, where the charge is four pence.

Some gentlemen congregated about the door at midnight are sure they saw a man and a woman, the latter being Mary Jane, stop to laugh at a poster on one side of the passage, which offers a hundred pounds reward for the Whitechapel murderer.

MARY KELLY WITH A STRANGER

ONE OF THE JACK THE RIPPER REWARD POSTERS.

The man must have enjoyed the joke, for he himself was the Whitechapel murderer beyond all doubt. This picture from real life of a murderer reading an advertised reward for his capture with the woman he is about to butcher, is not a usual one.

A great deal of speculation will be done as to whether he was a cold-blooded monster trembling at his own danger as he read, or a madman, defiant of everything and with difficulty restraining his impulse to kill at once.

The men who saw him can only say that he did not look remarkable.

DISCOVERY OF A VICTIM.
(Original 1889 Book Image)

THE FIEND CALMLY SURVEYS HIS BLOODY WORK.

THE FIEND CALMLY SURVEYS HIS BLOODY WORK.
(Original 1888 & 1889 Book Image)

At 10 o'clock in the morning, just as the Lord Mayor was climbing into his golden carriage, three horrified policemen, who had first looked in through Mary Jane's window and then drunk big glasses of brandy to steady themselves, were breaking in her door with a pickaxe.

BREAKING THE DOOR OPEN

The Whitechapel murderer had done his work with more horrible thoroughness than ever before.

The miserable woman's body was literally scattered all over her little room.

A description of such butchery is unpleasant to write, but is necessary to understand London's state of terror and to form an opinion as to this remarkable murder.

Almost every conceivable mutilation had been practised on the body.

McCarthy, the shopkeeper and landlord, had seen the body first. He had gone, as he had daily for a long time past, to ask for several weeks' arrears of rent, amounting in all to thirty shillings.

DISCOVERY OF THE MURDER AND THE CROWD THAT SOON GATHERED

Though not an imaginative man, McCarthy at once expressed the conviction that a devil, and not a man, had been at work.

This, by the way, is a new theory in regard to the murderer's identity.

The woman's nose was cut off and her face gashed.

She had been completely disembowelled, as had all the murderer's former victims, and all the intestines had been placed upon a little table which, with a chair and the bed, constituted all the furniture in the room.

Both the woman's breasts had been removed and placed also on the table.

Large portions of the thighs had been cut away, and the head was almost completely severed from the body. One leg was almost completely cut off.

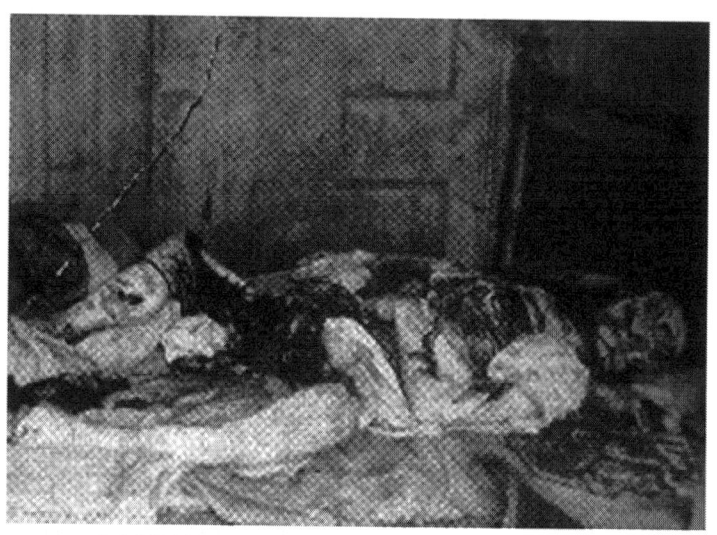

MARY KELLEY'S MUTILATED BODY.

The mutilation was so frightful that more than an hour was spent by the doctors in endeavouring to reconstruct the woman's body from the pieces, so as to place it in a coffin and have it photographed.

On the 8th of November, at midnight, Dorset Street and all the neighbourhood was swarming with such a degraded Whitechapel throng as have been already described in these columns.

Those with any money were getting drunk very fast.

The drunkenness of the poor of London is amazing.

Many sober women, and all the drunken ones, were crying from terror, while the men lounged about, singing or fighting and chaffing the women, according to their ideas of humour.

Gallantry is not rampant among these Whitechapel men.

The police were doing nothing of importance.

The poor woman's fragments, put together as skilfully as possible, were lying in the Houndsditch mortuary in a scratched and dirty shell of a coffin often used before.

The mortuary is in a graveyard back of the gloomy old Houndsditch Church, and not a pleasant spot late at night.

While the body was being carried from the scene of the murder, thousands crowded as near as the police would allow, and gazed with lifted caps and pitying faces at the latest victim.

The police did nothing but push the crowd about and be officious—this to such an extent that even those whose duty led them to the place found it necessary to place frequent softening half-crowns in policemen's palms.

The most interesting individual in Miller Court was a woman who had known the dead woman. Mary Jane's pal, she called herself.

Her room was directly opposite the murdered woman's and its agitated proprietor stood in the doorway urging a young girl with straggling wisps of red hair, who had started for beer, not to be gone a minute.

She assured a reporter that she would be glad to talk to him while Kate was away, just to forget the horrors.

This woman spoke well of the dead.

Her name was Mary, and she had not always been on peaceable terms with the murdered Mary Jane. Though quarrelsome, Mary Jane was pretty before she was cut up, she said, and she was only twenty-four, not thirty, as she looked: but she would fight, and did not care what sort of a place she lived in.

Mary's was about as big as a horse car. Sleeping and cooking were both done in it. On a clothes line stretched across it a night dress was drying. There was a bed one foot above the floor, a stool and a nondescript piece of furniture to hold things.

MARY'S ROOM IN MILLER COURT.

There was milk in a saucer on the floor, showing that vile air and worse drainage had brought the kitten down without the help of hunger.

When the girl with the red hair came back, the woman who had been a friend of Mary Jane drank in a few minutes a quart of beer, relating at the same time many incidents in the lives of herself and her dead friend.

At last, with a flood of drunken tears, she declared that she would never dare go out on the streets again to earn a living, observed somewhat inconsistently that lightning never struck twice in the same place, meaning that the murderer would never come back to Miller Court, made the red-haired girl swear an oath to stay all night, and went asleep on the bed with her head the wrong way up.

Those who think they have a working plan for reforming society should take a careful look through Whitechapel and see the things they have got to reform.

The girl with the red hair did not think it wonderful that no one had heard any sound of the murder.

Someone was always drunk and yelling in Miller Court, and she rightly guessed that a woman being beaten would make as much noise as one cut up, so that the murder would not be noticed.

For her part she was sure to imagine murder in every direction now.

She had a strong mind, however, had not had any beer, and did not cry. She knew positively that Mary Jane was alive at one o'clock, for at that hour she had heard her singing '*Sweet Violets*' to whoever was in her room.

This fact and the name of the tune has been solemnly entered in the police account of the case.

It is useless to theorize any further concerning the murderer.

He proved himself a man of wonderfully cool nerve or most utter recklessness.

(The following text is original to the 1888 version)

His cunning is displayed in having waited for the public terror to diminish and until the demands of Lord Mayor's Day should have called a great number of police from the murder-haunted district.

(End of 1888 text)

There is little prospect of anything resulting from the English detectives' efforts. London has resigned itself to wait till the murderer shall betray himself.

London has resigned itself to wait till the murderer shall betray himself,

(The following text is original to the 1888 version)

and is already wondering when the next killing will take place.

In consequence of the ninth murder, Sir Charles Warren, Chief of Police, baffled in all his efforts, resigned.

(End of 1888 text)

CHAPTER IX

WHO IS THE MURDERER?

The question faces us, who was the man who committed these harrowing murders?

Many explanations have been given.

"A suicidal maniac," says one.

"A crank afflicted with insane desire for notoriety," says another.

"A man who has been injured in some mysterious way by a woman of the unfortunate class, and who thus wreaks his vengeance."

One of the most palpable explanations given as to the identity of the murderer was that advanced by John Paul Bocock, in the New York '*World*,' ascribing the murders to Nicholas Vassili, a Russian, who committed a series of murders in Paris some years ago, and who, according to the journalist, now repeats his foul work in London.

Here is the story of Vassili's crimes.

Even if he should not prove to be the Whitechapel murderer, the story is interesting:

No stronger story of love, crime, fanaticism and mania has ever been told. The ferocious stamp of a savage realism marks the history of Nicholas Vassili from the first as that of a man unfettered from human restriction, a law, a creed, a passion unto himself. He was born in 1847, at Tiraspol, in the Province of Cherson.

At that time a religious reform was just beginning to stir from the timeworn ruts of their creed, the peasantry and middle classes of Southern Russia.

Nicholas grew up to feel its influence to the depth of his strange nature. He grew up to be a tall, stern youth, broad-shouldered, strong beyond the common power of his peers, dark eyed, pale-faced. His family were well to do; he did not have to work, but studied, pondered, and became before his majority an ascetic in body as in mind.

At the beginning of the year 1872, the Russian Church made a vigorous effort to repress the spread of this fanatical asceticism in Cherson, of which Vassili was now a leading exponent, and which seemed to be running havoc among the peasantry and middle classes. The sect of which he was the rising apostle was that of *'The Shorn.'*

When the Russian patriarchs began to persecute them, some of the Shorn were for a resort to arms. Others went into voluntary exile, and among the latter was Nicholas Vassili.

He was now twenty-five years of age and a notable-looking man in any assemblage. He had been well educated at Taraspol and at the University at Odessa, and he had inherited from his parents an income sufficient to his own frugal needs.

So fierce had been his denunciations of the oppressors of the Shorn, so vindictive his personal ascetism, that he had already come to be recognized as the young leader of this peculiar sect of the proscribed.

A WHITECHAPLE TYPE (Original 1888 Book Image)

Through him was crystallized and commanded for rigid discipline and observance of the main dogma, the cardinal principle of the creed, of the Shorn, which was the total abnegation of all fleshly (especially all sexual) pleasures. To this creed he deemed it his duty to convert the world. He gladly went into banishment, since it gave him an opportunity to make proselytes. The strength of his zeal had eaten up his human affiliations—he was no longer able to agree with even his fellow-sect-men.

He went to Paris, and made himself known through letters of introduction to several members of the Russian colony there. He did not desire new friends among them, but the opportunity through them of becoming acquainted with the city, with the people and with the cocottes. He had already devoted himself to the salvation of '*les ames perdues.*' He was now '*Der Seelenvetter.*'

In a month or two his new Russian friends saw him no more.

He could now find his way about alone.

He took bachelor lodgings in the Ruv3 Moufetarde. Here his tall, lean, brawny form, his pale, waxy face, his burning black eyes, soon attracted attention. He got to be known as an enigma.

Amid piles of books he worked away all day, and when night came went out into the streets to wander about until dawn. His new mission was big within him, but he had not yet revealed it.

Often his concierge would find him in the morning bent over his study-table, where she had left him the evening before.

By and by people began to talk of the '*Saviour of the Lost Souls.*'

He would be seen in the bright light of a cafe entrance, beneath the street lamps in the slums, at the edge of a dim *cul de sao* —wherever the '*nymphes du pave*' congregated or could be found by painstaking search—pleading with them, weeping over them, exhorting them to repent, lead a new life, save their souls and join the sect of the Shorn.

From entreaty he passed to malediction, and he would, in strange burning words and with uncouth gestures, draw pictures of the perdition to which they were hastening, and from which he begged them to permit him to save them.

Where they showed a sincere interest in his words, and promised to try to reform, he gave them money from his own purse. But his hopes for their reformation were uniformly disappointing.

A few nights would elapse, and the same painted faces and mocking eyes he had pleaded with and, he thought, partially reformed would present themselves to him under the gaslight and

laugh at '*the handsome gutter-preacher.*'

Whether they had cried or fled frightened, or only laughed at his earnest exhortations, the result was the same. He was unable to reform them.

He next made the acquaintance of a young lady who worked in a lace-making establishment.

Finally he realized that he, the leader of the Shorn, had fallen in love!

Then he tried to reconcile faith with passion, and besought Madeleine to become of his sect, to renounce the world and live for the conversion of her fellow-sinners.

She might even become his wife, in a spiritual sense only, and live and work with him. She demurred. He coaxed; then he threatened, and carried his point.

But no woman was ever won by threats.

And half ashamed of his own violence, Nicholas kept away from Madeleine for three days. He had never kissed her. Only a hand-clasp had sanctified the betrothal.

The fourth day he went to the apartment he had engaged for her in the Rue Serrurier.

The door was locked.

When he had knocked violently, Mme. Guidard, half frightened, opened her own door and asked him what was the matter.

"I don't know—I—where is Madeleine?" was all he could stammer out.

His face was frightfully distorted with a terrible presentiment " Madeleine went away," Mme. Guidard replied, "the day you were last here. She said you and she had got a home of your

own. Did she deceive me?"

Nicholas said nothing to this, but demanded that the apartment be opened.

"You see," went on Mme. Guidard, "she only removed a part of her wardrobe. She said you would come and take the remainder away for her."

Vassili fell into a chair and groaned.

Leaping up like a madman, he forced open the little desk he had given Madeleine, and ransacking its drawers, finally found what he had suspected, a note in Madeleine's handwriting, addressed to himself.

He stuffed her other letters into his pockets and sat down and read out to Mme. Guidard Madeleine's last words, which made a fiend of him:

"I thank you a thousand times for all your kindness. I respect but cannot love you. I am grateful, but why should I sacrifice all my life to my gratitude? That which brought us together separates us. You saved me, but you ought not to ask me as a reward. I cannot reconcile your roles of gutter preacher and lover. Forgive me and forget me!"

From that time on, Nicholas gave up his proselyting(1) and devoted his nights to a search for Madeleine.

His dagger in his bosom warmed his heart and promised him revenge for her scorn.

The only woman he had ever loved could not betray him with impunity.

After eight weeks he found her where he had first seen her, in the Rue Richelieu.

Without a word, he stabbed her in the back.

She fell at his feet with a scream.

He rushed off mumbling:

"She is saved forever; she is sure of heaven; she can sin no more now!"

Then the gutter preacher disappeared, and the Parisian police looked for him in vain.

A few days afterwards a cocotte was found in a quiet street of the Faubourg St. Germain, stabbed from behind, dead and mutilated.

Three days later another was found wallowing in blood, with the same wounds, in the Quartier Mouffetarde.

Tremendous excitement followed the discovery.

In a week another was found hacked and slaughtered in the same way.

Their money, purse, jewels, etc., were intact in all cases.

A panic such as that now in Whitechapel followed among the fallen women of Paris.

Nicholas, as he afterwards confessed, killed five of them in fourteen days.

One night in the Arrondissement of the Pantheon, a dark figure crept up behind a young girl, stabbed her and started to fly.

As she fell she turned and shrieked out, so that the police heard her:

"Nicholas Vassili!"

Then she died in Nicholas' arms, for he, too, had recognized her too late. He was seized, dragged to prison, and tried for murder.

His lawyer got him a fifteen years' sentence on the ground of insanity.

He confessed his murders to the jury, and told them of his mission on earth.

He regretted that he had not killed Madeleine when he first stabbed her, and when he left her, as he supposed, dying at his feet.

The bloody monster was released from the asylum in Tiraspol on January 1, 1888.

He was on his way to London when last seen in January.

The Whitechapel murders began in April, 1888.

Meanwhile "*Jack, the Ripper*" still lurks undiscovered.

After the ninth murder he sent out the following letter:

"Dear Boss: It is no good for you to look for me in London, because I am not there. Don't trouble yourself about me till I return, which will not be very long. I like the work too well to leave it long. Oh, that was such a jolly job, the last one. I had plenty of time to do it properly. Ha! Ha! The next lot I mean to do with a vengeance—to cut off their heads and arms.

You think it is a man with a black moustache. Ha! Ha! Ha!

When I have done another you can catch me. So good-bye, dear boss, till I return.

Yours,

"Jack the Ripper."

If he were the creature of a romance on the stage, the one immortalized by Stevenson as '*Dr. Jackyl and Mr. Hyde*," the murderer of Whitechapel could not play his double game to more

diabolical effect.

(1) Proselyting: convert or attempt to convert (someone) from one religion, belief, or opinion to another.

25. Sept. 1888.

Dear Boss

I keep on hearing the police have caught me but they wont fix me just yet. I have laughed when they look so clever and talk about being on the right track. That joke about Leather apron gave me real fits. I am down on whores and I shant quit ripping them till I do get buckled. Grand work the last job was. I gave the lady no time to squeal. How can they catch me now. I love my work and want to start again. You will soon hear of me with my funny little games. I saved some of the proper red stuff in a ginger beer bottle over the last job to write with but it went thick like glue and I cant use it. Red ink is fit enough I hope ha. ha. The next job I do I shall clip the ladys ears off and send to the

DEAR BOSS, LETTER PAGE 1

police officers just for jolly wouldnt you. Keep this letter back till I do a bit more work, then give it out straight. My knife's so nice and sharp I want to get to work right away if I get a chance. Good luck.

           yours truly
           Jack the Ripper

Dont mind me giving the trade name

wasnt good enough to post this before I got all the red ink off my hands curse it. No luck yet. They say I'm a doctor now ha ha

DEAR BOSS, LETTER PAGE 2

THE END.

H. H. HOLMES. AMERICA'S FIRST RECOGNISED SERIAL KILLER

While Jack the Ripper was terrorizing Whitechapel with his gruesome murders, another fiend was enjoying his own killing spree in Chicago. The name of this serial killer is H. H. Holmes, real name, Henry Herman Mudgett.

It is even thought by some that Holmes was responsible for the 'Ripper' slayings.

The story of Holmes is a fascinating read, and not only for those interested in serial killers and murders. Holmes actually designed and constructed a large hotel to entrap his victims, usually young defenceless woman, but men and also whole families. Included in the killer's hotel design were secret rooms, gas chambers, murder rooms and more.

Detective Geyer, the man responsible for revealing Holmes murders, wrote a book about the serial killer, which was published in 1896, and the original is now available in eBook format.

THE HUNT FOR H. H. HOLMES AND THE TRIAL OF AMERICA'S FIRST SERIAL KILLER

(Illustrated)

Book contains the full unabridged version of The Holmes Pitezel Case - A History Of The Greatest Crime Of The Century and the Search For The Missing Pitezel Children by Detective Frank P. Geyer, 1896.

Bonus material includes:

HOLMES CONFESSES 27 MURDERS

THE MOST AWFUL STORY OF MODERN TIMES

TOLD BY THE FIEND IN HUMAN SHAPE.

Every Detail of His Fearful Crimes Told by the Man Who Admits He Is Turning Into the Shape of the Devil. THE TALE OF THE GREATEST CRIMINAL IN HISTORY Copyright, 1896 by W.R. Hearst and James Elverson, Jr.

(Illustrated - complete and unabridged)

HOLMES' MURDER CASTLE

A Story of H. H. Holmes' Mysterious Work

By ROBERT. L. CORBITT. COPYRIGHT, 1895

(Illustrated - complete and unabridged)

WAS HOLMES JACK THE RIPPER?

www.benhammottbooks.com

Printed in Great Britain
by Amazon